T0305489

Digital Transformation

Digital transformation is a multidimensional concept and involves many moving parts. Successful digital transformation requires a fresh approach in harnessing people, process, technology, and data to develop new business models and digital ecosystems. One main barrier could be an overemphasis on applying technology to expand the business rather than transforming the people's mindsets to do things differently. Thus, it is important to develop a holistic view of these parts and assemble them to foster the right conditions for digital transformation to happen. Business leaders and executives must be equipped with a wide range of digital competencies to thrive in a rapidly changing digital environment.

Digital Transformation: Strategy, Execution, and Technology provides an overall view on the strategy, execution, and technology for organizations aiming to transform digitally. It offers insights on how to become more successful in the digital age by explaining the importance and relevance of the various building blocks which form the foundation of a digital organization. It shows the reader how to develop these building blocks in the organization as part of the digital transformation journey from both a business and technical perspective.

Highlights of the book include:

- Digital transformation strategy
- Digital governance and risk management
- Digital organization and change management
- Experimental learning and design thinking
- Digital product management
- Agile and DevSecOps
- Digital enterprise architecture
- Business applications of digital technology

This practical guide is written keeping in mind the needs of the business and information technology professional and digital transformation practitioners. It is also suitable for students pursuing postgraduate degrees and participants attending executive education programs in business and information technology.

Digital Transformation

Strategy, Execution, and Technology

Siu Loon Hoe

CRC Press
Taylor & Francis Group
Boca Raton London New York

CRC Press is an imprint of the
Taylor & Francis Group, an **informa** business
AN AUERBACH BOOK

First edition published 2023
by CRC Press
6000 Broken Sound Parkway NW, Suite 300, Boca Raton, FL 33487-2742

and by CRC Press
4 Park Square, Milton Park, Abingdon, Oxon, OX14 4RN

CRC Press is an imprint of Taylor & Francis Group, LLC

ISBN: 978-1-032-31795-3 (hbk)
ISBN: 978-1-032-11253-4 (pbk)
ISBN: 978-1-003-31139-3 (ebk)

DOI: 10.1201/9781003311393

Typeset in Minion
by SPi Technologies India Pvt Ltd (Straive)

Contents

Preface

The initial idea for writing this book emerged in early 2021, and the actual work began shortly after the proposal was approved by the publisher in the first quarter. The main challenge then was to ascertain the key topics to be covered in this professional book. Digital transformation covers a wide body of knowledge depending on the perspective taken. There are many interesting topics that are related to digital transformation, for example, digital transformation strategy, digital governance, risk management, change management, design thinking, digital product management, Agile, DevSecOps, digital enterprise architecture, and the different types of digital technologies involved. Taken from another viewpoint, these topics represent the basic building blocks that are necessary to be put in place by organizations wishing to enhance the probability of success in their digital transformation journey.

Thus, a broad-based book covering the basic building blocks for digital transformation will be valuable for those interested in this exciting and growing area. This book will provide an overview of selected topics that are relevant to digital transformation. The main purpose is to expose readers to a wide range of strategy, execution, and technology topics on digital transformation. It will be useful to introduce these different yet related ideas in a single book to managers and executives in both business and information technology roles, also to participants attending post-graduate or executive education programs to appreciate and understand the issues and practices involved. Readers will benefit from having a more holistic, organizational, and practice-oriented approach for digital transformation.

Acknowledgments

I would like to thank John Wyzalek, senior acquisitions editor, and the editorial and production teams at CRC Press for the assistance rendered. My special thanks to Nigel Wyatt for facilitating the proposal process and making the publication of this book a reality. Finally, I wish to express my deep and sincere gratitude to my family for their strong support over the years.

Author

Siu Loon Hoe is an associate professor of information systems (practice) and director of Master of IT in Business (Digital Transformation) program in the School of Computing and Information Systems at Singapore Management University. He teaches undergraduate and postgraduate courses in information systems and innovation, digital transformation strategy, and digital organization and change management. Previously, at the National University of Singapore, Siu Loon has delivered executive education programs in digital government and business process reengineering. He has also been a frequent speaker at the Lee Kuan Yew School of Public Policy.

Siu Loon has more than 25 years of industry experience in assisting C-suite executives from both the private and public sectors. He has held various senior managerial and consulting roles and has led large-scale change management projects across the region in China, Hong Kong, Malaysia, and South Korea. He was an invited forum speaker on investment in the healthcare industry organized by the United Nations Conference on Trade and Development (UNCTAD) and Association of Southeast Asian Nations (ASEAN) Secretariat.

Siu Loon obtained his PhD in management and MBA in international business from The University of Western Australia and BSc from the National University of Singapore. His works and commentaries have appeared in publications by Oxford University Press, Taylor & Francis Group, and Harvard Business Review Analytic Services. An award-winning reviewer and former associate editor of *The Learning Organization*, Siu Loon currently serves as editorial board member of *Journal of Information & Knowledge Management* and *Development and Learning in Organizations*.

Introduction

> When digital transformation is done right, it's like a caterpillar turning into a butterfly, but when done wrong, all you have is a really fast caterpillar.
>
> **George Westerman, MIT**

ABOUT THE BOOK

The growth of the global economy is increasingly powered by digital technologies. These technologies are changing the way how people live, work, and play. Digital technology advances such as cloud computing, Internet of Things (IoT) platforms, and big data analytics present numerous amazing opportunities for organizations. In addition, in a phygital world, organizations compete to create enhanced digital experiences for the customers. The prospect of engaging the customer at a higher level is an attractive proposition for organizations seeking business growth. Thus, organizations must embrace these digital innovations and transform the way they generate business value and operate to stay competitive. However, digital transformation is not without risks and brings with it many challenges. Although many organizations are already pursuing various digital projects, some may be grappling with issues pertaining to strategy, execution, or technology and may not be able to realize the full benefits from their investments.

Digital transformation is a multidimensional concept and involves many moving parts. Successful digital transformation requires a fresh approach in harnessing people, process, technology, and data to develop new business models and digital ecosystems. One main barrier could be an over-emphasis on applying technology to expand the business rather than

DOI: 10.1201/9781003311393-1

transforming the people's mindsets to do things differently. Thus, it is important to develop a holistic view of these parts and assemble them to foster the right conditions for digital transformation to happen. Business leaders and executives must be equipped with a wide range of digital competencies to thrive in a rapidly changing digital environment.

This book provides an overall view on the strategy, execution, and technology for organizations aiming to transform digitally. It offers insights on how to become more successful in the digital age by explaining the importance and relevance of the various building blocks which form the foundation of a digital organization. It shows the reader how to develop these building blocks in the organization as part of the digital transformation journey from both a business and technical perspective. This practical guide is written for the business and information technology professionals and digital transformation practitioners in mind. It is also suitable for students pursuing postgraduate degrees and participants attending executive education programs in business and information technology.

HOW THE BOOK IS ORGANIZED

The book is structured around three broad areas, namely, strategy, execution, and technology, that are relevant to successes in digital transformation. The eight main chapters or topics of the book are organized around these three areas. Under the strategy area, there is a chapter on digital transformation strategy. In the execution area, there are six chapters which include topics on digital governance and risk management, digital organization and change management, experimental learning and design thinking, digital product management, Agile and DevSecOps, and digital enterprise architecture. Finally, for the technology area, there is a chapter which covers business applications of digital technology.

Chapter 1 highlights the topic of digital transformation strategy and explains the strategic aspects of digital transformation. No digital transformation initiative would be successful without a well-thought-through game plan. The organization must have a blueprint of how the business can be augmented with digital technologies to stay ahead of competition. It is crucial to first develop a thorough understanding of the business challenges and gaps before applying the appropriate digital technologies to solve these problems.

Chapters 2 to 7 cover the 'execution level' topics. Organizations face many challenges and obstacles implementing digital transformation initiatives. Successful execution involves everyone in the organization rolling up their sleeves and performing the activities that achieve the key corporate and business goals. Executive management must adopt the right techniques and mobilize the entire organization toward the digital transformation vision. The various chapters will discuss these important topics related to the delivery of digital transformation initiatives and projects.

Chapter 2 is on the topic of digital governance and risk management. Digital governance seeks to strike a balance between conformance and performance. It involves a series of practices such as digital portfolio management, risk management, performance management, and data governance.

Chapter 3 features the topic of digital organization and change management. Organizations need a digitally ready workforce for digital transformation. To prepare for change, well-thought-out change management which covers stakeholder management, communication management, and training management is required.

Chapter 4 presents the topic of experimental learning and design thinking. Experimentations are important for the development of innovative digital products and services. A design thinking process which includes activities to empathize, define, ideate, prototype, and test will be useful.

Chapter 5 showcases the topic of digital product management. New products drive business growth. In the digital age, organizations require a mix of product and project management talents to succeed.

Chapter 6 describes the topic of Agile and DevSecOps. Agile practices address some of the shortcomings of the traditional waterfall method. DevOps brings together software development and IT operations activities with automation. When the security component is included, the set of practices is known as DevSecOps.

Chapter 7 is on the topic of digital enterprise architecture. A digital enterprise architecture helps to align business objectives and IT priorities, which improves decision-making. There are four domains that layer the overall digital enterprise architecture. They are business architecture, data architecture, applications architecture, and technology architecture.

Chapter 8 focuses on technology and has a write-up on the various business applications of digital technology. Technology is a key business enabler. While organizations may have access to similar technologies, it is the way that these technologies are applied that would differentiate them from competitors. Some of the digital technologies covered include artificial intelligence, big data analytics, IoT, wearables, augmented reality, social media, robotic process automation, and cybersecurity.

The conclusion chapter provides a wrap-up on the main ideas of the book. It also emphasizes that organization and individuals must always be ready to learn new digital competencies and adopt new mindsets to stay competitive in the digital age.

1

Digital Transformation Strategy

Every industry and every organization will have to transform itself in the next few years. What is coming at us is bigger than the original internet, and you need to understand it, get on board with it, and figure out how to transform your business.

Tim O'Reilly, O'Reilly Media

A TRANSFORMATION JOURNEY

Many people speak of the advent of the digital age, a time when there is widespread acceptance, integration, and use of digital technologies in the way we interact and transact. Digital practices would be so prevalent that businesses, governments, and societies cannot function properly without them. However, if one takes a closer look, the world has already undergone tremendous transformations brought about by mega technological change. Over the past few years, if an organization had not adopted some form of digital technologies to improve the business, it would be highly likely that it is in some form of trouble by now, or it is already out of business. For those organizations that have embraced digital technologies, the adverse market environment would have had a lesser impact on them, or they may even be thriving. To these tech-savvy organizations, the digital future is already here. In fact, some would even argue that the digital age has come and gone. The world is now in a post-digital age.

Despite the pervasiveness of digital technology, many organizations are still trying very hard to play catch-up to digitally transform. They continually scout for the latest digital technologies to match internal business requirements. Unfortunately, this technology-driven approach may not

DOI: 10.1201/9781003311393-2

5

yield the desired results. A digital transformation journey should not start with technology as a precursor (Tabrizi et al., 2019). It should begin with a holistic view of a business that leverages technology for competitive advantage. Organizations embarking on digital transformation must begin the journey with the business as the foremost consideration rather than from a technology standpoint. It is crucial to first understand the business challenges and gaps and then apply the appropriate technologies to solve these problems.

Depending on the extent to which the application of digital technologies changes the way of doing business, basic terminologies such as digitization and digitalization can be used to clarify and provide a better understanding of the notion of digital transformation. These terminologies do connote vastly different ideas because of the possible business value derived by the organization (Leinwand & Mani, 2021). At a basic level, digitization refers to the conversion of physical or analog documents to an electronic or digital form. It is a means to organize information to enhance information acquisition, recording, retrieval, dissemination, and storage. In most cases, digitization helps to lay the foundation for more complex and sophisticated approaches to transform the organization. As a result of digitization, the organization generally becomes more efficient. On the other hand, digitalization refers to an optimization of the organization's operating model using digital technologies (LeHong & Waller, 2021). The operating model is a representation of how the organization structures its core business processes to deliver value to customers and stakeholders. Thus, digitalization could mean changing current processes to provide new capabilities or enhance customer experience through technology. A good example would be using automation and business process management to improve productivity and customer interaction. The digitalization of core business processes and operations usually results in an increase in revenue produced or a reduction in cost from the existing lines of business.

Digital transformation is not the same as digitization or digitalization. It is not merely a change in the format of the documents used or an improvement made to the existing operating model to deliver value. Digital transformation is the creation of new business models by leveraging technologies (Hanelt et al., 2021; Spieth et al., 2014). This involves a total change in the business model and results in a complete makeover of how value is generated and delivered to the customers by the organization. The business model describes the relevant value creation activities of the organization to the customers and stakeholders. It includes components such as the organization's purpose, strategies, processes, organizational structure, infrastructure, modes of sourcing, product offerings, distribution channels, and partnerships. In this new way of doing things, the factors involved would not be its traditional form. There are fundamental changes being made to the business which go beyond operating at the efficient frontier. Through digital transformation, new products and services are made and the business is significantly scaled. As a consequence, new revenue streams are produced from the new products and services developed.

Perhaps the metamorphosis of a butterfly best encapsulates the idea of digital transformation. The butterfly metaphor provides a view of how a traditional business model can be changed into a totally new one. The worm-like caterpillar altering into a winged butterfly is a good illustration of digital transformation. Beginning life as a larva, a caterpillar would feed on leaves and spin a silky molt around itself. Within the cocoon, the hairy caterpillar radically changes its physical form and metamorphoses into a beautiful butterfly. The creature changes into a form that is totally unrecognizable from its original self. Similarly, the organization's new business model may also bear little resemblance to the traditional or old business model. The organization adopts a total change from the way it creates business value that is entirely different from what it has been doing all along. In addition, the caterpillar turned butterfly has also acquired a new flying capability and no longer needs to crawl from place to place. It is like the organization having developed new capabilities as part of the transformation.

Thus, digital transformation disrupts the traditional ways of doing business through new business model innovations enabled by digital technologies. A good example would be an organization using a technology or digital platform to connect multiple parties in an ecosystem and creating and delivering new forms of business value to all the stakeholders in a circular instead of a linear way. This business model change is a much broader concept compared to an operating model change which focuses solely on core business processes and operations to deliver business value. The organization brings together all the value-creating activities and interacts with multiple stakeholders in the ecosystem to preserve its competitive advantage. It goes beyond simply delivering business value but creates or generates business value in a totally different way. From this perspective, an operating model may be viewed as a subset of a business model. Of course, in practice, the boundary between a business model and an operating model is less clear.

The main purpose of highlighting the differences between digitization, digitalization, and digital transformation is to illustrate the extent to which the application of digital technologies transforms the way the organization does business and interacts with customers and the benefits involved. Nonetheless, digitization, digitalization, and digital transformation should be viewed as a continuous sequence of changes to the organization's assets, operating model, and business model resulting from digital technology adoption. These digital technologies may include mobile devices, smart sensors, cloud computing, and big data analytics. Digitization, digitalization, and digital transformation should not be regarded as distinct stages or discrete phases of change. After all, digital transformation is a journey of business innovation and growth.

In a related note, the digital transformation journey requires adopting a broader disruptive and change mindset by applying data, digital technology, and human-centered design to transform the business model. It is a shift in attitude or a new way of thinking on how digital technologies can create new business innovations and ideas. In addition, using human-centered design to ensure that the user's perspective in terms of behaviors, likes, and dislikes are factored into the digital products and services that truly meet human needs. An organization must rethink how it can solve complex problems by applying new methodologies and techniques. Through a realignment of strategy, people, process, technology, and data, the organization can alter the way it is run. It involves embracing new ways of doing business using new capabilities to serve customers. For example, the application of big data allows some organizations to derive valuable insights into customer issues, which were not possible previously. This will significantly enhance the decision-making process. Organizations that have a sound knowledge of both business and digital technology would be better poised to grasp market opportunities and overcome threats to create new business and operating models.

FROM TRADITIONAL TO NEW BUSINESS MODELS

Traditional business models rely on a linear and sequential way to create value. It is linear because the core business processes typically start with the suppliers and end with the consumers. The value chain or the series of activities generally includes procurement, production, distribution, and marketing. Traditional business models exist across many sectors and industries such as manufacturing, direct sales, and brick-and-mortar retailing. In the digital era, organizations that adopt a linear and sequential way to create value face many limitations and challenges. Scalability and resource allocation are major limitations of these types of traditional business models. As the customer base grows, the quantity of inputs required and the intensity of the processes needed to maintain a certain level of outputs also expand correspondingly. In other words, the more customers there are, the more resources and a higher degree of work activities are needed to meet increasing demand. To illustrate, take the case of a traditional transport company. With an increase in the demand for commuting, more vehicles are needed, and these must be purchased. Also, more labor is required to manage the increased customer bookings. Consequently, the ability to scale is constrained by factors such as the availability of funds for the purchase of additional vehicles, the current number of vehicles owned by the company, the current number of drivers available, and the recruitment rate and training slots available for new drivers.

A key challenge faced by organizations that operate traditional business models is the increasing competition from non-traditional players. These new entrants are not the conventional market players which the organization is familiar with or expects to see. These organizations face contenders coming from totally different industries and sectors. The pervasiveness of digital technology has enabled new competitors that have the advantage of direct access to customers and their buying patterns to penetrate traditional areas and compete directly with the incumbents. They develop products and services that span traditional industry boundaries and pose a big challenge to the incumbents. They can do so because of their deep customer and supplier knowledge. For example, many financial services and insurance organizations face intense competition due to the disaggregation of financial services brought about by fintech companies or new technology startups with an extensive customer reach and the ability to scale their offerings. As the current players are not digital natives, they are unable to compete effectively in a digital world. Consequently, there will be disruptions to the business leading to profit erosion.

An alternative form of business model could help organizations address the issues of scalability and resource allocation and fight competition. In this different form, the organization could rely on a circular and continuous way to create value for all the parties involved in the transactions. Consider a ride-hailing company that uses a digital platform to match private vehicle drivers seeking passengers with commuters looking for transport to places. This new business model relies on the circular flow of demand and supply between private car drivers and commuters to ensure that the needs and wants are met. As the number of commuters seeking car rides increases, more new private drivers could join the digital platform to offer their services and vice versa. In this scenario, the company operates without the constraints of having to own any physical assets such as vehicles because it is digitally enabled and functions as a matchmaker that brings different parties together for a commercial purpose with a fee. The company creates business value by balancing the needs of the two sides using a digital platform. Take another example of a media company. Traditionally, the company sells information services to readers. As an alternative form of business model, the company could connect writers and advertisers with readers. In doing so, the media company widens the user base and integrates the offerings to different users. It is no longer constrained by the volume of information services or contents that it can create which limits its growth potential. Of course, there would be investments required to build a digital platform and overheads incurred to maintain the infrastructure and also, to increase the engineering and customer service manpower. However, compared to the traditional business model, these types of new business models allow for greater scalability and flexibility for exponential growth opportunities.

These types of new business models bear various interesting characteristics. Firstly, they utilize a network view of the digital world powered by data. The network view arises because of the increasing complexity of government, business, and societal relationships, and new market opportunities offered by digital technologies. In this new business model, organizations could tap on collaborative networks powered by new technologies and data to create and deliver value that is very different from the old ways of doing things. For example, with the widespread adoption of digital technologies, there are many opportunities for online transactions. The internet is a powerful medium where people can search for information, compare prices, and transact. The amount of information available on the internet is growing at a phenomenal rate. A lot of analysis and insights could be derived from the information provided by different parties. With better insights, more products and services could be offered to targeted audience.

Secondly, these new business models allow access to assets or products without the need for actual ownership. Organizations and individuals are no longer required to own the assets to be able to use or derive benefits from them. Take the examples of short homestay accommodation and electric car sharing. Airbnb does not own the properties but simply matches the hosts and guests for the homestay. Also, the electric car drivers do not need to own the actual vehicles but rent them on-demand based on a fixed rate. Thirdly, because the organizations or customers do not necessarily own the actual assets or products themselves, the services provided are usually experience-based. In such instances, the consumers may be spending money just to try out a new experience or an innovative product. Space travels fall within this category. There are several explanations for this phenomenon. One explanation is that people may be bored of doing the same routine activities, so they find new avenues to break the monotony. Another reason could simply be that they value stimulations of the senses more than material possessions.

DIGITAL PLATFORMS AND ECOSYSTEMS

Organizations that employ new business models capitalize on providing real-time information and all-day availability of products and services to their customers. The backbone for these new business models is a digital platform that supports online and real-time connection with all the stakeholders in an ecosystem. This digital platform is the interface with business rules, mechanisms, tools, and activities for the diverse group of participants. It makes it much easier for sellers to reach new customers and vice versa. In the ecosystem, the organization links up the communities and helps them resolve issues collaboratively with one another. The digital platforms and ecosystems business model fuses the digital and physical worlds, making collaborations faster and transactions cheaper.

As the boundary between the physical and digital world becomes less clear, an organization could reap a lot of benefits by creating an integrated end-to-end experience for the customers and by connecting them to different parties. The digital platform model is made possible because of the pervasiveness of the internet which enables connectedness and facilitates communication. A key advantage of the digital platform model is that it reduces market inefficiencies and allows the business to scale exponentially. In addition, a digital platform model enables the organization to operate in a different industry because of the customer insight that can be derived from a digital platform. In such a platform business model, the main aim is to connect different groups of users (Chakravorti & Chaturvedi, 2019). For example, the organization could be creating an ecosystem which provides circular and continuous services for the different stakeholders.

Basically, a digital platform is a collection of bundled software and hardware that utilizes large data sets to provide digital services. It serves a diverse group of users and is accessible by a wide range of digital devices. Through a defined set of rules, the digital platform enables collaboration of which some may be the provision of goods and services between various parties. The users could also build their own applications on top of the digital platform. The activities that are centered around the digital platform are mostly transactional in nature. Consumers could buy products and services through searches and reviews. Suppliers could promote their merchandise and solution in the same way. Through a digital platform which connects the stakeholders, the organization could synchronize demand and supply of products and services. In addition, it could also market their brand of products and services on the digital platform. In effect, the organization benefits from the digital platform by matchmaking consumers and providers with a service fee. Furthermore, it takes advantage of the digital platform to sell its own merchandise or services. In the process, the organization gathers a tremendous amount of information about the customers and suppliers. With this new knowledge and insights gained from the customers, more offerings could be provided, thereby, further deepening, and widening the customer relationship.

In the digital world, a high degree of competitive advantage could be gained through partnerships and development of an ecosystem (Agrifoglio et al., 2020; Kane et al., 2019). An ecosystem is a community of participants not controlled by the organization that manages the digital platform. For example, they could be a group of consumers and suppliers or application developers and technology companies. The ecosystem provides an environment for the different groups to interact, collaborate, and transact. There are a few ways where organizations can work with their partners to tap into an existing ecosystem, for example, creating new products and services, providing new customer interactions, and accessing new distribution channels. Alternatively, organization can also form new ecosystems such as a new marketplace to match buyers and suppliers, and a collaborative network of partners offering an end-to-end service.

In most cases, a digital platform forms the foundation for all the stake-holders to interact and create business value for the customers. For those organizations that are already managing an ecosystem with a digital plat-form, the challenge would be to continually improve the offerings by enhancing the total user experience of the digital platform, for example, by shortening the turnaround time from the point of product selection to payment and physical delivery of the product on the digital platform. The entire customer journey should be seamless and delightful. This would sig-nificantly boost repeat visits and retention of customers. In the case of a digital product, a simplified workflow should be designed to ensure error-free download and installation. Essentially, the organization should review all the organization's key touchpoints with the customer to make sure that customer needs and expectations are met or exceeded. The development of a digital platform is not an easy task and may take years to realize any prof-its; the main challenge is still the creation of a viable business model that brings together strong partnerships within a healthy ecosystem.

Network effects play a big role in a digital platform business model (Hagiu & Wright, 2020). The idea behind this is that the value of a plat-form increases for everyone when more participants join in. The number of users in a network is important because most of the value are derived from the users. For example, when more suppliers sign up in a digital mar-ketplace, the range of offerings is widened, and consumers have more choices to select from. Similarly, when more potential customers register with the digital platform, sales should increase resulting in high revenue and profitability for the suppliers. Likewise, in a social networking service setting, an increase in the number of members leads to more users joining because they see the benefits of joining a bigger community which allows greater connectivity.

The structure of networks is determined by the number of classes of users it serves. In a one-sided market, there is only a single class of users. Consider a digital platform which operates a business for consumers. There is only a single class of users, namely the buyers. The interactions are only between the sole platform operator and the buyers. In a two-sided market, the platform delivers benefits to two distinct classes of users. An auction platform is a good example. There are both suppliers and buyers in this marketplace. The digital platform functions as an intermediary creating value from the transactions generated by the two classes of users. It is a simple and convenient way to bring people together. Digital platforms can also serve multi-sided markets where more than two classes of users interact and do business.

In a two-sided market, the classes of users may display a preference regarding the number of users within the same class or in the other class. If the users are within the same class, the phenomenon is referred to as same-side effects. On the other hand, if the users are in the other class, it is known as cross-side effects. The increase or decrease in the classes of users has varying results which can be either positive or negative. For example, in a marketplace platform, an increase in the number of sellers is viewed positively by the buyers because there are now more product choices available to them. From the buyers' perspective, this is a positive cross-side effect since the sellers belong to the other class of users. However, from seller's point of view, it is considered a negative same-side effect because the increase in the numbers of sellers, which is from the same class, raises competition and may lower sales.

STRATEGY DEVELOPMENT

In the early days of digital transformation, organizations are mainly concerned with optimizing internal processes using digital technologies. The emphasis is on cost reduction which tends to be more inward looking and defensive in nature. These organizations hope that by improving operational processes and eliminating waste, they can better compete in the market. The digital transformation trend has shifted somewhat to an externally focused strategy such as developing partner networks and growing the customer base. There is now more thought given to building ecosystems with stakeholders that are supported by digital platforms (Atluri et al., 2018). The aim is to look outside the organization to capture a bigger market share with new products and services. To increase customer retention and attract more customers, many organizations have tried to improve the transaction logic based on human-centered design to significantly improve the overall customer experience. The goal is to be better connected with the customers and provide them with enhanced or new experiences.

With rapidly changing digital technologies and fast-evolving business models, organizations need a well-crafted strategy to navigate the business environment and compete with other players. However, a sound strategy goes beyond producing the required outputs in a strategic plan. Although important, these outputs are just prerequisites for a coherent strategy and are not sufficient to guide the organization into unknown territories, especially in the digital age. A commonly missing piece in a strategy is a clear set of choices that define what the organization is going to do and what it is not going to do. The set of predetermined choices is crucial because it limits the options available and keeps the organization focused on the key result areas. It helps to channel all the efforts into activities that are critical to the success and survival of the organization. Only with bounded options would the organization be able to execute the strategy without any distractions and make tasks manageable.

The strategic planning function is closely related to strategy development. Strategic planning is the practice of prioritizing choices and determining the necessary actions to bring the organization forward into the future. As part of the strategic planning process, the chief executive officer (CEO) would set the direction for the organization and develop key strategies for business growth. The first step usually involves an evaluation of the current state of the organization. The executive management team would take a step back from its day-to-day operations to critically examine its current performance. Next is to determine where the organization aspires to be in the future. The team should visualize what a digital future would look like and establish the digital capabilities needed to achieve this ambition. Finally, to decide what needs to be changed, generate creative ideas to transform the business, and develop actionable plans.

In a typical strategic planning exercise, an organization would define its vision, mission, goals, and actions. In addition, other outputs such as core values, SWOT (strengths, weaknesses, opportunities, and threats) analysis including competitive advantage, initiatives, and financial projection are also produced. Each of these outputs which form part of a strategic plan will be briefly explained. Particularly, the topic on shared vision will be elaborated because of its high relevance to digital transformation initiatives. A vision is a statement of the end point which the organization hopes to arrive at. It is a vivid picture of the future and what a successful organization looks like. It is not simply a slogan or catchphrase but a credo to rally the organization. The main purpose of a vision is to paint an ideal picture of the future to inspire the organization to push forward in a certain direction. This vision seeks to appeal more to people's feelings than to reason. Thus, it may represent an ideal state that may not be fully achievable. Nonetheless, the vision gives hope and challenges everyone to give their best efforts. It provides motivation to everyone in the organization to go to work every day. The phrasing of the vision statement should be simple to understand and memorable.

An important consideration in any digital transformation initiative is how to focus the collective energies of people in the organization toward a future state. One approach in which the executive management team could lead change and engage the people is the development of a shared vision for the digital future. A shared vision occurs when members of the organization identify themselves with this future state. The shared aspect of the vision statement is an important feature because individuals are personally committed to the vision. The executive management team does not need to exert any additional effort on the organization to marshal it to move in that direction. Employees are not compelled or forced to comply with it. It is entirely voluntary because employees are inspired by the shared vision statement and identify with it. Employees do it because they want to, not because they have to. In general, most individuals would like to be committed to something that is much larger than themselves.

Well-crafted shared visions serve to inspire the organization and motivate employees to reach the end point (Vaz, 2021). A shared vision helps to galvanize employees toward a common goal. The process of creating a shared vision should lead to a rethinking of the way the organization behaves and is structured. It should generate some organizational tensions because there is now a gap between the organization's existing state and the desired state. This tension could serve to direct organizational efforts to close the gap. Consequently, the organization would need to change its business or operating model to transform into the new form. This may lead to a reorganization of the units and activities to deliver value to the customers.

Through a shared vision, employees can make better sense of the direction the organization is going despite seemingly varied actions of others. It can help to bring together individuals with different approaches to work in a synergistic way. The reason is that a shared vision confers a sense of consistency to sometimes conflicting operational and administrative activities. In any organization, workplace conflicts are bound to arise from the daily activities. However, since the employees already have a sense of the end state, they can choose and decide on the means to achieve the end. They are empowered to act within the broad parameters set by the organization to achieve the business goals. A shared vision focuses on the where to go and leaves the how to do it to the individuals to discover for themselves. From this perspective, the organization shifts from a control to a commitment mode to drive success. Driving digital transformation initiatives by galvanizing employee commitment is far more effective than using a command-and-control style of management.

A mission statement describes how the organization can achieve the end state and is the reason why the organization exists in the first place. A strong mission statement builds commitment, loyalty, and motivation among the employees (Anthony et al., 2019). The goals specify what needs to be accomplished especially when the organization needs to make major transitions. Goals are often cascaded to the next lower level known as objectives. Objectives are more specific in terms of being measurable and quantifiable. They are also more short-term in nature. Core values are the set of principles and fundamental beliefs to guide the organization to work toward its goals. They provide guidance for day-to-day operations and serve to steer employees to drive business and financial growth. A SWOT analysis is a means for the organization to look critically at itself. It draws on four perspectives to assess the organization's internal and external factors and potential. Initiatives are key action programs formulated to improve business performance. Finally, the financial projection is a forecast of future revenues and expenses. It also contains the budget for the proposed programs.

Once these key outputs have been determined by the executive management, the next step is to help the various levels of the organization to take ownership of the business goals. Typically, off-site meetings and workshops are held with executive and middle management. The mission, vision, and organizational targets would be presented, and the respective units would also share their annual business and support plans to achieve these goals. Upon executive management approval, the teams would then proceed to execute the activities and report on the progress periodically.

There are some strategic planning good practices that can help the organization make the process more efficient and effective. Firstly, the strategic planning team should represent a broad spectrum of functions within the organization. Besides those senior-level executives who report directly to the CEO, the team should also include high potential managers from other functions such as operations, marketing, and information technology (IT). Secondly, the strategic planning process could be designed as a sequence of short activities which collectively and progressively build on the sections of the strategic plan rather than a long and intensive exercise. Thirdly, for implementation, the organization should communicate the strategic plan to all levels of the staff as well as external stakeholders such as customers and alliance partners. Fourthly, the strategic planning outputs must be integrated with the organization's regular business review routines and the progress monitored. Finally, to recognize and reward employees who contribute to the key initiatives. For example, incentives such as performance bonuses could be tied to the achievement of the agreed outcomes. Doing so helps to reinforce ownership of the goals and plans and sustains the momentum for strategy execution.

IT CAPABILITY ENHANCEMENT

Digital transformation is a journey, and a strong foundation is needed to bring the organization to a higher level of performance. Many organizations rush into digital transformation initiatives without first addressing the fundamental business issues and IT problems. Prior to embarking on a full-scale digital transformation exercise, it is important to first close the existing business gaps and resolve any underlying process inefficiencies. Then, the organization can focus on the basic building blocks such as IT capabilities and build upon them in a systematic manner. IT capabilities focus on how technology brings business value and contributes to the overall success of the organization. As part of the strategic planning process, the IT function would need to develop its own separate and logically connected objectives to support organizational and business objectives. The overall strategic plan serves as the basis to guide the development of the IT plan. The output is an IT plan which is vital in supporting the digital transformation strategy.

The IT plan is a core aspect of the organization's digital transformation strategy and needs to be aligned to the strategic plan. It provides the blueprint for the management of IT to support the organization's operations and enable digital transformation. To develop an IT plan, an initial IT risk assessment should be conducted to ascertain the corresponding threats to any proposed digital transformation initiatives. The IT risk assessment must comprehensively highlight the challenges, complexities, and worst-case scenarios. A risk mitigation plan could then be developed with proposed measures to address IT development and implementation issues. This should take into consideration the existing digital enterprise architecture and current disaster recovery practices. The executive management should be directly involved in driving the IT plan that is associated with the new digital transformation initiatives. One practical approach is to constitute a digital governance committee comprising of selected members of the executive management and key business and support unit representatives. The digital governance committee should oversee all matters that are related to IT portfolio management, risk management, performance management, and data governance.

An IT plan typically covers the following areas: strategic and business objectives, IT capabilities, IT trends, IT structure and responsibilities, enterprise architecture and roadmap, operational support, IT initiatives, and IT budget. The strategic and business objectives are derived from the strategic plan. IT trends cover existing and emerging technologies that have an impact on the organization from a business perspective. IT structure and responsibilities are an outline of the human resource component and depict the IT organization structure and digital competencies of the staff. The enterprise architecture and roadmap cover a high-level overview of the business, data, application, and technology layers. It also defines the current and desired future state of IT assets. Operational support is a description of the list of IT services provided to the organization, for example, network security and helpdesk support. IT initiatives are the list of IT programs and projects to be implemented. Metrics and indicators linked to the organizational initiatives are included as well. Financial management is an important component of IT strategy which consists of an IT budget. The IT budget covers the flow of IT project funds and how it contributes to the organization's financial health.

A critical area which the organization should focus on is its capabilities or collection of skills and expertise. These are the intangible assets which represent how people and resources are organized to accomplish the key business and digital transformation activities (Davenport & Redman, 2020). In the digital domain, it translates into digital and IT capabilities. Some examples of IT capabilities include employees with the necessary technical skills and expertise to develop digital platforms, clear and well-defined IT roles and responsibilities, the required processes and systems are in place to manage IT risks, and the executive management's passion to drive digital transformation. As a result of the technical nature of digital platforms, the IT function becomes a natural fit to manage and operate them. Consequently, strong IT skills and expertise are required to design and implement a digital platform. For example, the IT team must have strong system integration and data science competencies. Some of the other domains of expertise that are needed include cloud management, distributed Internet of Things (IoT), and digital experience. Cloud management deals with the type of cloud services used and its resource allocation while distributed IoT enables the suite of software residing on physical devices to operate seamlessly. Digital experience is concerned with the set of technologies that give users a consistent, secure, and personalized access across different touchpoints. IT capabilities are the result of organization's investments in talent management, human resource training and development, communication, and compensation. Such IT capabilities must be linked to the overall strategies to drive the organization forward.

CASE ILLUSTRATION

As new business and operating models continue to emerge and evolve, it is a challenge to pinpoint exactly how a successful organization should function in the digital age. There are many factors to be considered and evaluated. Nonetheless, there are currently many organizations that exhibit characteristics that position them well to thrive in the digital world. These organizations apply digital technology to analyze customer data and develop digital platforms and ecosystems to create new customer experience and business value.

One example is Grab. Grab first started as a ride-hailing company aimed at offering safe taxi rides for passengers and shortening the existing taxi booking process (Grab, n.d.). The app was built essentially to manage the supply of taxis as well as passenger demand for taxis. It operates as an intermediary and does not own any vehicles. Grab has since evolved from being a transport company to offering mobility, deliveries, and financial services through an all-in-one app. Its partners include private hire drivers, food delivery drivers, F&B merchants, market merchants, and payment merchants. Grab's business and operating model also changes in response to the needs of partners and customers. Grab continues to strengthen its digital platform to connect merchants that sell a wide range of daily essentials to customers who enjoy a seamless user experience while using the app. As the number of users grows and frequency of usage increases, more customer insights can be gathered to cater to new products and services. A network effect occurs as the offerings gain additional value because more customers use it. In the next stage of development, a Grab consortium has been awarded a banking license to build Singapore's next-generation digital bank.

SUMMARY

This chapter highlights the importance of first understanding the business challenges before applying the appropriate digital technologies to solve these problems. It discusses the notions of digitization, digitalization, and digital transformation. The limitations of traditional business models versus new business models are also explained. Digital transformation results in an organization transitioning into a new business model usually supported by a digital platform serving an ecosystem. Network effects are an important factor in building an ecosystem. A strategic plan and IT plan are useful to set the direction for the organization and prioritize the actions for digital transformation. Determining the strategic choices is an important aspect of the strategic planning process. As part of the digital transformation strategy, organizations should emphasize the people side of change and develop IT capabilities. Developing a shared vision helps to align teams and individuals toward a common digital outcome. Also, building up the internal IT capabilities of the organization is an ongoing activity in the digital transformation journey.

REFERENCES

Agrifoglio, R., Lamboglia, R., Mancini, D., & Ricciardi, F. (2020). *Digital business transformation: Organizing, managing, and controlling in the information age* (1st ed.) Springer International Publishing. https://doi.org/10.1007/978-3-030-47355-6

Anthony, S. D., Trotter, A., & Schwartz, E. I. (2019). *The top 20 business transformations of the last decade*. Harvard Business Review. https://hbr.org/2019/09/the-top-20-business-transformations-of-the-last-decade

Atluri, V., Dietz, M., & Henke, N. (2018). *Competing in a world of sectors without borders*. Digital McKinsey Insights. https://www.mckinsey.com/business-functions/mckinsey-analytics/our-insights/competing-in-a-world-of-sectors-without-borders

Chakravorti, B., & Chaturvedi, R. S. (2019). *Ranking 42 countries by ease of doing digital business*. Harvard Business Review. https://hbr.org/2019/09/ranking-42-countries-by-ease-of-doing-digital-business

Davenport, T. H., & Redman, T. C. (2020). *Digital transformation comes down to talent in 4 key areas*. Harvard Business Review. https://hbr.org/2020/05/digital-transformation-comes-down-to-talent-in-4-key-areas

Grab. (n.d.). *Our story Grab Sg*. https://www.grab.com/sg/about/

Hagiu, A., & Wright, J. (2020). *When data creates competitive advantage and when it doesn't*. Harvard Business Review. https://hbr.org/2020/01/when-data-creates-competitive-advantage

Hanelt, A., Bohnsack, R., Marz, D., & Marante, A. (2021). A systematic review of the literature on digital transformation: Insights and implications for strategy and organizational change. *Journal of Management Studies*, *58*(5), 1159–1197. https://doi.org/10.1111/joms.12639

Kane, G. C., Palmer, D., Phillips, A. N., Kiron, D., & Buckley, N. (2019). *Accelerating digital innovation inside and out: Agile teams, ecosystems, and ethics*. MIT Sloan Management Review. https://www2.deloitte.com/za/en/pages/digital/articles/accelerating-digital-innovation-inside-and-out.html

LeHong, H., & Waller, G. (2021). *Digital business ambition: Transform or optimize?* Gartner, Inc.

Leinwand, P., & Mani, M. (2021). *Digitizing isn't the same as digital transformation*. Harvard Business Review. https://hbr.org/2021/03/digitizing-isnt-the-same-as-digital-transformation

Spieth, P., Schneckenberg, D., & Ricart, J. E. (2014). Business model innovation – state of the art and future challenges for the field. *R & D Management*, *44*(3), 237–247. https://doi.org/10.1111/radm.12071

Tabrizi, B., Lam, E., Girard, K., & Irvin, V. (2019). *Digital transformation is not about technology*. Harvard Business Review. https://hbr.org/2019/03/digital-transformation-is-not-about-technology

Vaz, N. (2021). *Digital Business transformation: How established companies sustain competitive advantage from now to next*. John Wiley & Sons.

2

Digital Governance and Risk Management

The biggest part of our digital transformation is changing the way we think.

Simeon Preston, FWD Insurance

BALANCING CONFORMANCE AND PERFORMANCE

Corporate governance is concerned with the set of practices and processes used to direct an organization (Ebert et al., 2020). It covers a broad scope including environmental awareness, strategy, and ethical behavior. Corporate governance serves to balance the need to achieve economic goals without sacrificing social goals. A key challenge is to optimize the trade-off between compliance and performance. While excessive controls hinder progress, a lack of restrictions would lead to statutory breaches and financial losses. The board of directors is charged with the responsibility of creating and preserving wealth for the stakeholders while ensuring transparency, accountability, and security. Together with executive management, they help to set up decision rights and accountability, and establish governance policies aligned to business objectives. The organization then closely monitors investment returns and risks in accordance with the guidelines set.

Digital governance is an integral part of corporate governance. With the rise of digital technologies, organizations are developing more and more digital and electronic assets such as digital currencies and digital payment methods. Thus, digital governance would have to take into consideration these digital assets beyond the traditional information technology (IT) assets such as hardware and software. In such a digital setting, the board directors and executive management are be faced with many strategic

DOI: 10.1201/9781003311393-3

questions that are related to IT performance in the organization. For example, 'How well is the organization harnessing digital technologies to enable the core business?', 'What are the business value and benefits derived from the various digital transformation initiatives?', and 'What is the organization's action plan to prevent cyber-attacks and protect digital assets?'. These are all pertinent issues because IT plays a very important and strategic role in business. The responses to this list of strategic IT questions fall within the purview of IT or digital governance.

Digital transformation and IT initiatives generally require significant investments and have relatively high risks. In some cases, the returns obtained from these digital initiatives fall short of expectations. Due to the technical nature of digital initiatives, they frequently do not receive the amount of attention they deserve from the board directors and executive management. A lot of the strategic IT decision-making is left to technical committees and senior IT officers. To address these concerns, closer board supervision and executive management involvement and examination are needed (Caluwe & De Haes, 2019). The board of directors should drive this alignment taking into consideration the balance between maintenance and expansion needs of the organization (Liu et al., 2019; Turel et al., 2019). The parties must focus on business and IT alignment to create business value (Chau et al., 2020; Gregory et al., 2018). The expectations and performance measurements should be spelled out clearly, so that IT resources can be focused in the right areas. At the same time, they should proactively manage enterprise risks to make sure that they are consistent with the expected returns from these IT resources, and also to put in place risk mitigation measures to safeguard the interests of the organization.

Digital governance involves the leadership, organizational structures, and processes that enable IT to meet the organization's strategies and objectives. The organization must be able to run a robust IT operation along with key digital governance practices, such as digital portfolio management, risk management, performance management, and data governance in place. With greater clarity of the digital governance structure, roles, and processes, the organization would be able to make faster decisions and move quicker in the market. Broadly, the executive management should determine all the digital initiatives within a digital portfolio and align them with business goals, and then, ascertain their risks and returns, cascade the plans and goals down the organization, and measure their performance (Ajjan et al., 2016). For this to happen, the executive management team needs to take an enterprise-wide view of risks to articulate the potential impact on business outcomes. They should also set up processes to monitor the progress of these digital initiatives. Furthermore, the organization must also be cognizant of contemporary IT practices, such as Agile and digital product management. These innovative IT practices introduce new norms and behaviors to the digital product and service development process. To stay relevant, the modern organization must ensure that these practices are an essential part of digital governance when designing and developing policies and procedures.

DIGITAL PORTFOLIO MANAGEMENT

One of the key challenges faced by organizations is the assessment of the value of their digital investments (Maizlish & Handler, 2005). The construction of a digital portfolio is the first step in addressing this issue. With a digital portfolio, the organization would be able to have a comprehensive view of all the digital initiatives that are happening. This overview helps to reduce the number of redundant and overlapping digital projects in the organization. The idea of portfolio management originated from the world of finance and economics. The notion is to group assets into different classes such as equities, bonds, and cash and assign them different degrees of risk and return. The concept and its applications were later carried over into product portfolio planning and IT budgeting. Regardless of the disciplines, the main objective is to optimize the risk and return to meet business goals. There are various benefits associated with a robust digital portfolio management framework, Firstly, it serves to present a holistic view of the total digital investments and benefits derived, leading to more effective funding decisions. Secondly, it helps to achieve an optimal IT mix by balancing higher risk, higher reward digital projects with safer, lower reward ones. Thirdly, with greater transparency over funding allocations, it improves alignment and communication across business and support functions.

There are different methods of categorizing digital investments. For example, one of the techniques is to group digital initiatives or digital assets into four categories, namely, transactional, informational, strategic, and infrastructure assets (Weill et al., 2002). The transactional category refers usually to systems which automate repetitive activities to improve efficiency. For example, this category could include ticket reservation and billing systems. The informational category covers systems that manage, comply, and analyze information such as payroll, revenue management, and tax reporting systems. The strategic category confers the organization some competitive advantage in the market which it operates in. These strategic systems provide a distinct advantage to the organization when it comes to producing goods that can be launched more quickly compared to the competitors. One good example is a just-in-time inventory management system between a manufacturing company and its key suppliers. Another similar method is to categorize IT assets into strategic, operational, and compliance projects. Based on this view, the strategic category would cover mostly business-value-creating digital projects such as those that transform the business model while the operational category comprises operational and infrastructural projects, and the compliance category includes projects that are mandated by regulators or government agencies. The strategic category could also be sub-categorized to cover projects which optimize the business and includes digital projects that support functional areas to improve efficiency and effectiveness. In the end, there would be four categories of digital initiatives or digital projects, namely, strategic, optimization, operational, and compliance. From these two illustrations, it is evident that a digital initiative or digital project can be categorized in a variety of ways depending on the purpose it serves. An important categorization criterion is the main contribution of the digital initiative toward the strategy and business case. For example, while a digital project or system may have operational components but if the main motivation for embarking on the digital project is to lay the foundation for a new operating model to engage new customers, then it should be categorized as optimization as described in the second method.

Once the digital projects have been categorized, they could then be put into a digital portfolio. Using the example of the four categories of digital initiatives, namely, strategic, optimization, operational, and compliance mentioned previously, the categories could be further hypothetically described as follows. The strategic category is created for digital projects or systems meant to give the organization a competitive advantage through the implementation of innovative digital products and services. Such digital products and services may be part of a new digital platform which engages external stakeholders in a totally different way. Some examples include the shift to a new digital platform that supports an ecosystem to better understand customer behavior or the introduction of Internet of

Things (IoT) sensors, which collect important environmental information and provide new digital services to customers. The strategic category of digital projects would be associated with innovation and market leadership type of initiatives. The organizations championing strategic projects are mainly early adopters of digital technologies striving to build new business models to transform the business or industry. They are generally more innovative in developing new digital products and services and are very agile in their operational processes. Nonetheless, in a highly competitive market environment, it would only take a few years before competitors catch up and level the playing field. Thus, what was once a strategic project may no longer be able to sustain market leader's dominant market position after a while. When this happens, the once strategic project would have to be re-categorized into an optimization or even operational project.

The optimization category comprises digital projects or systems that enhance an organization's performance in terms of improving business process efficiency and effectiveness. They cover system development projects and upgrades to improve service response time and information management. Very often, optimization projects have a specific business outcome such as reducing customer response time, increasing accessibility for users, and providing more options for virtual collaboration among employees. They are usually linked to specific business initiatives. An optimization project could involve application developments to increase productivity, functional enhancements to enhance customer experience, or knowledge management to improve the quality of decision-making. Some examples of optimization projects include enhancements made to order processing, accounts payment, inventory control, and report generation systems. Since optimization projects mainly focus on the automation of laborious and repetitive activities, and the redesign of core tasks with the assistance of digital technologies, they generally 'sit on top' of the basic systems in the operational category to help them to function optimally.

In many organizations, the operational category consists of a large group of day-to-day systems such as mission-critical applications, shared services programs, utility networks, security modules, and infrastructure. This category covers the administrative systems, hardware, and software used to run the internal operations of the organization. They are essential in supporting the operational tasks of internal stakeholders but do not necessarily give rise to any competitive advantage for the organization. Some examples of these operational projects include basic administration of human resource and financial management systems, standardization of system features, consolidation of hardware, and integration of software. Most of these digital projects do not directly link to any specific business initiative but are a fundamental requirement in supporting and maintaining the efficiency of other systems. Thus, areas such as network connections, internet access, and facilities management would also fall into this category.

Finally, as the compliance category name implies, compliance projects are related to systems which control the activities that help an organization comply with statutory or legal requirements. Some of these examples are systems dealing with anti-money laundering, credit card risk, personal data privacy, and disaster recovery. As these are all mandated by the regulators and government agencies, organizations are required to conform and the spending on these projects is non-discretionary by nature.

RISK MANAGEMENT

In a volatile, uncertain, complex, and ambiguous (VUCA) environment, managing risk should be a significant part of an organization's business activities. The risks identified should include both business and technology risks. Enterprise risk management adopts a strategic perspective of the entire organization in identifying, managing, and monitoring risks. All the risks associated with an organization are no longer identified and managed in silos but enterprise wide. It is a useful approach because some enterprise risks may not necessarily be applicable to specific business units but would have a major impact on the overall organization. The key staff involved in the enterprise risk management process are mostly executive management or C-suite executives. They may include the chief executive officer, chief financial officer, chief operating officer, chief risk officer, chief information officer, business unit heads, and support unit heads.

A risk management process typically includes the identification, evaluation, and monitoring of risks. Risk identification is the step in which the risks that could potentially prevent the organization from achieving its objectives are picked out. There are a variety of risk identification techniques such as through interviews, questionnaires, and external benchmarking. From these activities, a list of risks would be generated. The general types of risks include strategic risk, operational risk, and financial risk (Vincent et al., 2017). Strategic risk is related to the external environment and market conditions. The external environment is affected by numerous political, socio-economic, and regulatory forces. Some of these examples are protectionism, economic slowdown, changes in consumer preferences, and data protection requirements. Strategic risk could also include reputation risk, legal risk, and succession risk. Operational risk is related to the organization's processes, technology, and people. They may include a lack of business continuity planning, inadequate testing before implementation of new systems, use of unlicensed software, and inadequate staff induction and training. Financial risk comprises credit risk and liquidity risk. There could also be risks arising from volatility in foreign currencies, interest rates, and commodities. In identifying financial risk, the organization would need to consider factors such as the strength of asset and liability management, adequacy of cash inflows, and exposures to foreign currencies. In the context of digital transformation and digital governance, there is also a need to pay special attention to and understand technology risk. Technology risk is mainly due to disruptions to the business as a result of technology failure. A simple illustration is a negligent employee falling prey to a password leak due to phishing or a stolen personal computing device. Consequently, the organization may face financial losses due to the exposure of confidential data or damages to its reputation because of disruptions to the IT systems.

Once the risks have been identified, the next step is to associate each of the identified risks with a possibility category of it happening and the potential impact if it happens. The possibility category is also known as the likelihood of occurrence. The likelihood of occurrence could be based on a qualitative ranking of possibility categories such as high, medium, and low. For example, a 'high' rank may suggest that the risk identified is almost certain to occur within the next six months unless it is controlled; a 'medium' rank may suggest that there is some likelihood of the identified risk occurring at least once in the next one year unless controlled; and a 'low' rank could imply that the identified risk could occur at least once in the next one to three years. Similarly, the identified risks would also be assigned a qualitative impact category, that is, high, medium, and low. In this case, a 'high' could result in catastrophic damages to the organization's reputation while a 'medium' could lead to negative consequences to the organization; and a 'low' as having minimal consequences overall. The next step is to prioritize the various identified risks in a risk matrix ranging from insignificant (low) to significant impact (high) on the x-axis, and low to high possibility on the y-axis.

Referring to the hypothetical digital portfolio, which was constructed earlier, each category of digital projects could then be assigned an occurrence and impact profile. For example, the risk associated with the strategic category would normally be classified as 'high'. The reason is obvious since digital projects that are in this category usually involve the application of emerging digital technologies in new and untested markets. Due to uncertainties such as the level of market acceptance, it is extremely difficult to forecast the demand and potential profitability for these projects. In addition, strategic projects tend to have higher operating costs and negative impact on return on investment (ROI) initially. It would be a big challenge in trying to monetize value creation in the early stages of these projects. Organizations may also face internal resistance in launching strategic projects. There could be a lack of willingness of employees to adapt to the new processes and changes. On the other hand, the return associated with strategic projects would usually be classified as 'high'. The competitive advantages that could be gained may include new lines of business, better market positioning, and innovative product leadership. All of which would give rise to increased revenue and profitability.

The level of risk that comes with the optimization category is 'moderate' because the digital technologies applied are generally mature and the new processes adopted established by nature. Through major process improvements using digital technologies, significant benefits such as transactional cost reduction and manpower savings can be realized. The optimization category is more likely to yield good financial outcomes such as a better ROI. It should have a positive effect on revenue, cost, speed, or service. The level of return is also expected to be 'moderate'. It should be noted that the monetization of returns should not be the main motivation for optimization projects. Rather such projects should be viewed as attempts to achieve other long-term organizational capabilities. Consequently, this category of the digital portfolio should be measured against other corporate key performance indicators (KPIs) and not just the ROI alone.

Digital projects in the operational category tend to consume a significant amount of resources. However, they tend to ride on established technologies and processes, which means that the risk is generally 'low'. Since these basic administrative systems and infrastructure projects do not generate much business value, the return generated would be 'low'. Nonetheless, it is important to note that the true value of operational projects lies in lowering the overall costs of IT operations and increasing efficiency while enabling strategic and optimization projects to meet key business goals. Finally, the compliance category is special because these digital systems are a pre-requisite for the organization to operate. It is a regulatory requirement to have these digital projects to keep the organization going. Thus, given its mandatory status, one could classify both its levels of risk and return as 'low'. In the next step, these categories would be linked to the identified risks and business strategies in the performance management process (Bainey, 2016).

Risk management is an integral feature of business and corporate governance. The objective is not for the organization to operate the business in a risk-free environment. Rather, it is to acknowledge the inherent risks involved, identify actions to mitigate these risks, and proactively deal with them from a strategic standpoint. With the assignment of the likelihood of occurrence and impact, and prioritization of the identified risks, executive management would proceed to assess them. A risk management plan would normally involve four types of action or strategy, namely, to avoid, reduce, transfer, or accept the risk (Öbrand et al., 2018). In certain situations, an event would have a high possibility of occurring, leading to substantial financial losses. In such cases, it may be more prudent to avoid this risk. For example, in view of the political and economic uncertainties in a target market, the organization may decide to postpone the launch of key products in that market until the environment improves. Under conditions where an event may have a high likelihood of occurrence, but with limited financial impact, the organization may opt to reduce the risk by implementing various control measures. For example, due to the risk arising from cost fluctuations of raw materials, the organization may decide that the contract terms and conditions with suppliers in the event of price changes are stated explicitly and more specifically. To transfer risk is to share the risk with another party. A straightforward example is the purchase of property insurance to protect the organization's physical assets from damage due to fire or theft. Finally, in some scenarios, the organization may have no choice but to accept the risk, for example, investing in an emerging technology in an untested market. Very often, there are many unavoidable risks when doing business. There may be no choice but to accept certain risks in exchange for future business growth and profitability.

Risk management is an iterative process which requires the setting up of various initial risk parameters. More importantly, there should be continuous efforts in monitoring and reporting of risks as part of corporate and digital governance. At the executive management and board levels, risk reviews fall under the purview of C-suite officers and audit committees, respectively. Regular risk monitoring and periodic risk reviews must be incorporated in the overall risk management process. Other related activities involve checking or surveillance on key risk areas. A major challenge facing many organizations is to recognize that risk management should be a value creation rather than a control process. Instead of focusing and checking what could go wrong, risk management practices should be designed to help the broader set of stakeholders identify areas where they can add value to the inputs received and convert them into higher quality outputs which derive superior benefits. To elaborate on the nature of value creation, risk management activities, for example, could help to bring about greater clarity on the responsibilities between stakeholders, identify innovative services, discover new markets and customers, and allocate resources more efficiently. Finally, constant communication and consultations with both internal and external stakeholders should be maintained throughout this process (Edirisinghe & Pinsker, 2020).

PERFORMANCE MANAGEMENT

Many organizations find it a challenge to justify the business value for digital transformation and define its success. There is a lack of consensus on how to measure the ROI. This is understandable because new business models are generally untested, and there are a lot of uncertainties regarding their eventual success. Furthermore, digital transformation initiatives always involve high upfront IT development and infrastructure costs. For example, building a digital platform requires a tremendous amount of resources. Consequently, the rate of digital transformation among organizations is much slower than expected. Thus, there is a need to actively manage the performance of digital transformation initiatives.

Performance management is a process where the organization monitors and evaluates its accomplishments in achieving its strategic and financial objectives. In the process, the setting of KPIs is an important activity. These KPIs should measure the outcomes as a result of the changes made to the major business drivers. The purpose is to assess the areas of the organization which require improvement when the desired result is not achieved. Thus, KPIs should be specific to certain aspects of the organization and be actionable. Different categories of KPIs such as financial and non-financial should be considered. There exists a myriad of KPIs to track and analyze the financial health of the organization. These KPIs include measures of profitability, liquidity, solvency, and valuation. Without proper KPIs, both executive and middle management would have problems managing the various digital transformation activities and reporting on the progress.

A combination of strategic and tactical KPIs to assess different dimensions of digital transformation could be developed. For instance, one set of KPIs could cover customer experience in utilizing the digital platform. Customer experience is crucial in a 'phygital world' – a blend of the physical and digital world. It is the basis for increasing the customer base and retention. Some examples of these KPIs are the number of new customers acquired and the number of repeat customers. Another set of KPIs could be used to measure the financial impact of digital transformation. These are the more traditional KPIs such as revenue increase, ROI, and cost of customer acquisition. Employer satisfaction is another important dimension of digital transformation. Thus, KPIs such as employee adoption rate of the new digital platform and productivity gained could be developed to appraise the change management program. It is crucial to view digital transformation as a journey to improve organizational culture and the overall business model. In this regard, the organization may wish to consider other KPIs to promote workplace interactions. For example, KPIs to measure agile practices adoption, experimentation of new concepts, and cross-functional collaborations. Finally, these KPIs should be tied back to staff performance bonuses and incentives to motivate everyone in the organization to strive ahead.

The balanced scorecard (BSC) is sometimes used by organizations to measure performance from a more holistic standpoint (Kaplan & Norton, 2001). The BSC is an approach to organize, structure, and communicate strategy using strategy maps, objectives, measures, and targets. It covers four perspectives, namely, financial, customer, internal processes, and learning and growth. The financial perspective is based on the successes from a shareholder's standpoint. These financial measures include revenue, cost, profitability, ROI, and economic value-added. The customer perspective takes a customer's view in the form of achieving the organization's vision. Some popular customer measures are market share, customer satisfaction, and customer retention. The internal processes perspective seeks to look at business process excellence to satisfy the customers and shareholders. Some of the popular measures include efficiency, cost, speed, and quality. Finally, the learning and growth perspective looks at the organizational capability that is essential for the organization to perform the activities well. These measures cover employee productivity and employee satisfaction.

Through a series of cause-and-effect relationships, the BSC is linked to the organization's strategy, creating separate strategy maps. Together with a mix of performance drivers and outcome indicators, the causal paths would eventually lead to the financial objectives. Once the BSC framework has been set up, the organization could then monitor both its current financial, customer, and internal processes performance, and its efforts to improve activities, employees, and information systems from a learning and growth perspective. Similarly, with the business objectives, measures, targets, and initiatives established in a BSC, the IT systems and digital projects could also be linked to the various initiatives. In this way, there is a close correlation between these IT systems and digital projects and the actual business initiatives. The BSC would form the basis for prioritizing initiatives and setting up of a target portfolio where IT systems and digital projects and desired business outcomes are clearly linked.

Like private sector organizations, public and social sector organizations also need to achieve financial KPIs as part of performance management, for example, keeping operating costs low. However, they are generally more concerned with achieving their mission and meeting the needs of their constituents than the financial objectives. A common approach for performance management that is used by government and not-for-profit organizations is to identify and map the inputs, activities, outputs, outcomes, and impact of a project or program. This approach centers on specifying all the necessary conditions required to bring about a given long-term change. Briefly, inputs refer to the resources such as manpower, funding, and physical assets that are required for an initiative. The activities are the series of tasks or work needed to convert resources into the desired outputs. The outputs relate to the tangible objects produced from the conversion of resources through the various work activities. The outcomes refer to the end results or consequences arising from the delivery of the outputs. Finally, impact describes the ultimate, sizeable goal brought about by positive and lasting change. Based on this logic flow, KPIs could be developed to monitor the progress of the projects and evaluate the results. Using this approach, public and social sector organizations could link any IT systems and digital projects to business projects to manage performance.

DATA GOVERNANCE

With the pervasive use and proliferation of data, there should be an established set of policies and procedures on the acquisition, utilization, and safe keeping of these assets. One feature of data is that it is cross-boundary. This means that the same set of data may be used by different people within an organization regardless of the departments which they are from. Similarly, these data may also be handled by different parties such as vendors and contractors who are outside of the organization. Therefore, it is imperative that organizations step up their efforts to proactively manage and protect data.

Data management practices aim to ensure that the organization uses its data assets to meet the strategic objectives both efficiently and effectively. Data management covers a wide range of activities such as data creation and access, data storage options which may be either in the cloud or on-premises, data availability, application of data in different software, data privacy protection and security, and data retention (DAMA International, 2021). Specifically, the domains involve data architecture, data modeling and design, data storage and operations, data security, data integration and interoperability, documents and content, reference and master data, data warehousing and business intelligence, metadata, and data quality.

Data governance serves to establish the roles, responsibilities, and processes for ensuring accountability for and ownership of data assets. It supports data management domains by determining the decision rights for the data-related processes. Thus, data management and data governance go hand in hand. In establishing a set of digital governance policies and actions for the organization, some of the areas that should be covered include the organization's vision and mission, key focus areas, data rules and definition, decision rights, accountabilities, control mechanisms, data stakeholders, data governance office, data stewards, and data governance processes. A formal data organization structure which establishes the official reporting relationships that manage data assets should be instituted. Some of these roles include the chief data officer, data governance council, data stewards, data manager, data custodian, and data user.

For organizations embarking on a digital transformation journey, the areas of data governance and protection cannot be over-emphasized. The reason is that the risk data breach is significantly increased due to greater exposure in cyberspace. For example, a digital platform is very vulnerable to remote access attacks. Consequently, valuable customer and employee data may be lost or stolen. To mitigate such situations when they arise, organizations should plan and ensure that data are appropriately anonymized such that they cannot be identified to individuals. Furthermore, to introduce measures to safeguard these data through encryption and tokenization. Of course, data governance and protection mechanisms such as data classification, access rights, and data transfer requests among others should also be established.

CASE ILLUSTRATION

The Monetary Authority of Singapore (MAS) recently updated the set of technology risk management guidelines for the nation's financial sector (Monetary Authority of Singapore, 2021). These guidelines contain technology risk management principles and best practices for financial institutions. It defines the roles of the board of directors and executive management for technology risk governance and oversight. It also contains other information such as a technology risk management framework for risk identification, risk assessment, risk treatment, and risk monitoring, review, and reporting.

Development Bank of Singapore (DBS) Group Holdings Ltd was the winner of the Singapore Corporate Awards' inaugural best risk management award (Tay, 2019). DBS was first established in 1968 with the responsibility of financing the country's young and growing industries (Development Bank of Singapore, 2018). In 1998, it became the largest bank in Southeast Asia and the largest retail bank in Singapore. The award recognizes the bank's effort in leading risk management practices to sustain its business in a time of rapidly changing digital technologies. The award criteria include the extent of disclosure on technology governance. Beyond developing the necessary IT policies and risk management processes, DBS has provided more training programs to upgrade the digital competencies of their people.

SUMMARY

This chapter highlights the importance of digital governance in a modern organization. Digital governance seeks to strike a balance between conformance and performance. Some of the key aspects of digital governance are discussed. These practices include digital portfolio management, risk management, performance management, and data governance. Digital portfolio management is beneficial to the organization because it provides a comprehensive view of all the digital initiatives that are currently being run. Risk management activities typically include the identification, evaluation, and monitoring of risks. It is an iterative process that requires the setting up of risk parameters and continuous efforts in monitoring and reporting of these risks. Performance management is a process where the organization monitors and evaluates its accomplishments in achieving its strategic and financial objectives. Both financial and non-financial key performance indicators should be used in the evaluation. Data governance involves the establishment of a set of policies and procedures on the acquisition, utilization, and safe keeping of these assets. It is a crucial part of digital governance.

REFERENCES

Ajjan, H., Kumar, R. L., & Subramaniam, C. (2016). Information technology portfolio management implementation: A case study. *Journal of Enterprise Information Management*, *29*(6), 841–859. https://doi.org/10.1108/JEIM-07-2015-0065

Bainey, K. (2016). *Integrated IT performance management*. CRC Press. https://doi.org/10.1201/b19231

Caluwe, L., & De Haes, S. (2019). Board level IT governance: A scoping review to set the research agenda. *Information Systems Management*, *36*(3), 262–283. https://doi.org/10.1080/10580530.2019.1620505

Chau, D. C. K., Ngai, E. W. T., Gerow, J. E., & Thatcher, J. B. (2020). The effects of business-IT strategic alignment and IT governance on firm performance: A moderated polynomial regression analysis. *MIS Quarterly*, *44*(4), 1679. https://doi.org/10.25300/MISQ/2020/12165

DAMA International. (2021). *DAMA-DMBOK: Data management body of knowledge* (2nd ed.). Technics Publications.

Development Bank of Singapore. (2018). *DBS: The 50 years*. Development Bank of Singapore. https://www.dbs.com/livemore/uploads/DBS-The-50-years.pdf?pid=sg-group-pweb-about-slideupbanner-dbs-the-50-years

Ebert, C., Vizcaino, A., & Manjavacas, A. (2020). IT governance. *IEEE Software*, *37*(6), 13–20. https://doi.org/10.1109/MS.2020.3016099

Edirisinghe, V. N., & Pinsker, R. (2020). IT risk management: Interrelationships based on strategy implementation. *International Journal of Accounting and Information Management*, *28*(3), 553–575. https://doi.org/10.1108/IJAIM-08-2019-0093

Gregory, R. W., Kaganer, E., Henfridsson, O., & Ruch, T. J. (2018). IT consumerization and the transformation of IT governance. *MIS Quarterly, 42*(4), 1225–1253. https://doi.org/10.25300/MISQ/2018/13703

Kaplan, R. S., & Norton, D. P. (2001). *The strategy-focused organization: How balanced scorecard companies thrive in the new business environment.* Harvard Business School Press.

Liu, P., Turel, O., & Bart, C. (2019). Board IT governance in context: Considering governance style and environmental dynamism contingencies. *Information Systems Management, 36*(3), 212–227. https://doi.org/10.1080/10580530.2019.1620508

Maizlish, B., & Handler, R. (2005). *IT portfolio management step-by-step unlocking the business value of technology* (1st ed.). John Wiley & Sons.

Monetary Authority of Singapore. (2021). Technology risk management guidelines. https://www.mas.gov.sg/-/media/MAS/Regulations-and-Financial-Stability/Regulatory-and-Supervisory-Framework/Risk-Management/TRM-Guidelines-18-January-2021.pdf

Öbrand, L., Holmström, J., & Newman, M. (2018). Navigating Rumsfeld's quadrants: A performative perspective on IT risk management. *Technology in Society, 53*, 1–8. https://doi.org/10.1016/j.techsoc.2017.09.009

Tay, P. G. (2019). Best risk management ingredients: Policies, processes, technology, people, and culture. *The Business Times.* https://www.businesstimes.com.sg/hub/singapore-corporate-awards-2019/best-risk-management-ingredients-policies-processes-technology

Turel, O., Liu, P., & Bart, C. (2019). Board-level IT governance. *IT Professional, 21*(2), 58–65. https://doi.org/10.1109/MITP.2019.2892937

Vincent, N. E., Higgs, J. L., & Pinsker, R. E. (2017). IT governance and the maturity of IT risk management practices. *The Journal of Information Systems, 31*(1), 59–77. https://doi.org/10.2308/isys-51365

Weill, P., Subramani, M., & Broadbent, M. (2002). Building IT infrastructure for strategic agility. *MIT Sloan Management Review, 44*(1), 57–65.

3

Digital Organization and Change Management

> You can't delegate digital transformation for your company… You and your executives have to own it! Executives need to engage, embrace, and adopt new ways of working with the latest and emerging technologies.
>
> **Barry Ross, Ross & Ross International**

A DIGITALLY READY WORKFORCE

We live in a world where digital disruption is commonplace and is constantly on everyone's lips and mind. Technological change is inevitable regardless of one's industry or sector. The recent pandemic has accelerated the pace for digital transformation. Overnight, millions of people across industries transitioned from working in the office to working from home. The crisis has also sparked new waves of innovation with an increased use of digital technologies for workplace collaboration and operations. Thus, organizations must continue to develop digital capabilities to support the future workplace and grow a digitally ready workforce.

An organization must explore new ways of doing things and harness digital technologies to stay ahead of competition. For example, the organization may choose to 'stay close' to the customers and become a digital organization. In other words, to be where the customer is to be able to better understand their buying patterns and engage them using the most convenient and attractive digital platform. The organization would also take full advantage of mobile devices and social media to offer round-the-clock information and immediate digital services. Internally, the organization could provide clearer segregation on the types of work most suitably performed by humans and machines, for humans, jobs which require

DOI: 10.1201/9781003311393-4

building relationships and strategic thinking. The latter type of work would concentrate on repetitive and onerous tasks. In the event of major disruptions to business operations, the employees would be able to continue working virtually from the comforts of their homes. All aspects of the organization's operations could be easily delivered digitally online and with minimal startup costs.

Very often, when businesses and governments refer to digital transformation, the emphasis is on 'digital' rather than 'transformation'. Technology seems to take precedence. While it is all right to harness digital technologies for innovation, it is the people who would make things happen through business model changes. For an organization to be successful, the workforce must be developed with the right digital mindsets and be equipped with digital competencies (Bashir & Miyamoto, 2020). At the basic and intermediate levels, digital literacy skills could include a fundamental understanding of mobile devices, coding, social media, and internet platforms. For the more advanced skills, these could cover more technical areas in cybersecurity, artificial intelligence, and Internet of Things.

Traditionally, employees in a department specialize in an area of work and build deep know-how within it. They are called I-shaped people because of their depth of knowledge. Then, there are the T-shaped people who are required to solve problems that are complex and interconnected to other areas. T-shaped employees have the advantage of being able to see issues from a different perspective and are generally more adaptable under different situations. These individuals are particularly valuable in managing the integration of information from diverse domains. Thus, I-shaped people who already have deep expertise in a specific field are expected to step up and be able to do other things well too. Cross-training becomes increasingly important for I-shaped employees to be developed into T-shaped employees. However, in the digital world where the boundaries between virtual, physical, IT, and business world are blurred, people are encouraged to become Pi-shaped employees. These individuals not only have broad-based skills, but they also have deep expertise in two or more domains (Sage-Gavin et al., 2019). These employees are highly competent individuals because they can combine the knowledge gained from a science, technology, engineering, or mathematics (STEM) subject with a business function such as finance or a domain such as logistics.

Organizations need to invest more time and effort to design digital career road maps for employee job matching to prevent skill obsolescence. Digital talent management practices which include talent acquisition, management, development, and retention processes should emphasize digital competencies. In addition, these processes should be supported by digital human resource management tools (Strohmeier, 2020). There should also be stronger ownership from the operating units and tighter integration with the human resource function for employee training and development. For example, career development for digital talents should include mentoring, coaching, attachments, exchanges, role modeling, and succession planning. Also, staff deployment for digital transformation projects should closely match with the digital competencies required.

TRANSFORMING THE WAY PEOPLE THINK AND ACT

In a constantly evolving business environment driven by shifting consumer preferences, digital technologies offer many exciting opportunities for organizations to solve age-old problems and overtake their competitors. Advances in new digital technologies provide business solutions once thought impossible. However, introducing technological change into an organization is a totally different ball game. Although the digital transformation plan may look perfect on paper, embedding the change in an organization would require significantly more effort. It is not just about the technology itself but the need to understand how people respond to change as well. Thus, organizations must be proactive in tackling the challenges which come with the introduction of change. The most common mistake is a lack of emphasis on the human side of change. When introducing new technologies to an organization, addressing technical problems usually takes precedence over people issues. This is understandable because there are many technical challenges to be overcome during implementation, for example, software integration and cyber security issues. Nonetheless, digital transformation is primarily a form of cultural change where people transition from traditional way of doing things to a new way of operation.

Organizations are run by people. Thus, people are the most important asset because they make things happen. Change must be managed well as part of the overall digital transformation journey. Very often, organizations speak of people being their most important asset. However, whenever change is introduced to the organization, people-related issues are not being properly addressed. One main reason could be that employees are expected to be 'professional' and simply act on the tasks rationally and without any personal emotions involved. A common blunder is to espouse a 'I tell, you do' mentality to change without addressing the genuine concerns of the employee. Very often, it is because of emotional rather than rational reasons that people object to change. Thus, it is crucial to let people understand and accept the need for change. Organizations must focus on transforming people by inculcating a digital mindset and developing digital competencies (Orduna, 2021). A digital mindset involves keeping an open mind in using digital technologies and data to solve business problems. Consequently, organizational change management must take a central role in digital transformation. A digital transformation program must take into consideration the 'soft-side' of change, that is, the people aspect.

An organization must have the capability to manage change. As digital transformation requires orchestrating different organizational pieces such as strategy, process, people, technology, and data for it to work, enlisting the 'right' people with the 'right' competencies to take on the roles of change leaders and managers are crucial. This group of change agents should have the leadership capabilities, business acumen, and technical skills to accomplish the tasks. They must be able to develop a high-level view of the business problems, engage the stakeholders to deliver the digital solutions, and implement new processes. For example, a change manager may have to present a business case or convince fellow colleagues of new ideas. The other skills that are important include people management skills, communication skills, and conflict management skills. Finally, for organizational change to occur, the employees must be engaged, empowered, and aligned to the digital transformation initiative. To achieve this, the organization must develop robust plans to engage the key stakeholders, manage communication, and deliver relevant training.

FUNDAMENTALS OF MANAGING CHANGE

In the initial stages of the digital transformation journey, the organization should consider issues such as developing a vision for change, identifying sources of resistance, and providing change leadership and executive management support. Developing the vision for change involves thinking through the narratives for digital transformation. The intention is to invoke a sense of purpose to motivate the whole organization toward a common goal. Resistance to change can be minimized if the root causes are identified and actions taken early to address the issues. Change leadership and executive management support are needed in areas such as stakeholder management, communication management, and training management (Tang, 2019). Stakeholder management attempts to group interested parties according to their organizational power and influence on the project and seek to understand their concerns regarding digital transformation. Communication management looks at the informational needs of the target groups and strives to provide timely and relevant information to ensure transparency. Training management is concerned with developing the employees' knowledge, skills, and attitudes for digital transformation.

An effective change management program serves to maximize the investments in implementing a digital transformation initiative. There are a variety of change management approaches and frameworks to guide the organization to planning, leading, and managing change. Some of the more popular frameworks include Kotter's eight-step model, which highlights variables such as urgency, coalition, vision, communication, short-term wins, and momentum (Kotter et al., 2021) and the ADKAR model which represents the elements of awareness, desire, knowledge, ability, and reinforcement (Hiatt, 2006). Lewin's idea to unfreeze, change and refreeze is often used as a conceptual model for change management practices (Rosenbaum, More, & Steane, 2018). These tools are very useful references to analyze the gaps in the people side of change and develop a change management plan as part of the organization's digital transformation journey. A change management plan typically includes a vision and case for change, key stakeholder management, communication management, training management, and sustaining culture change over the longer term.

Many organizations embarking on a digital transformation journey fail to provide a compelling reason as to why the business needs to do so. The reasons and value for digital transformation are not well articulated, and most of the employees do not understand the purpose of the change. Digital technology is a means to an end. Therefore, it is important to first explain the business problems clearly and then highlight how digital technology can help to close the gaps. Doing so will allow the employees to better appreciate and understand why the organization is going digital. As an example, an initiative to convert physical documents into an electronic format should not be viewed merely as a digitalization exercise but as an effort by the organization to better engage the customers in a timelier manner. Consequently, the leadership and executive management must give more thought and effort in explaining the purpose of digital transformation. This is because once the 'why' is made clear and internalized by the employees, the 'what' and 'how' become intuitively easier for middle management and the rank and file to implement the digital transformation plan. In a complex and uncertain environment, it is impossible to predict and anticipate certain scenarios from happening. A clear and well-explained purpose serves to provide some guidance in uncharted waters. Once people understand the reason for change, they will be empowered to explore different ways to achieve the outcome without being bogged down by unnecessary details.

A major challenge faced by organizations embarking on digital transformation is to justify the anticipated benefits. While it may be easier to calculate the costs involved, quantifying the benefits is far more problematic. Maintaining the status quo is always less costly because of the marginal costs involved in running existing IT systems. If the business does not convincingly show any positive results, then the impetus for change is weakened. Thus, the scales are tipped in favor of no change from the very beginning. Consequently, it becomes more difficult to convince people especially the skeptics about digital transformation. To overcome this hurdle, it is important to explicitly state both the potential tangible and intangible benefits, and whenever possible, assign a dollar value to these benefits. General categories of benefits include achieving higher speed, lower cost, and better quality. Examples of benefits are savings gained from a reduction in multiple data entries and re-keying errors. When data is captured once at source, there is no need to manually re-key the data again later. This not only saves valuable manpower but also prevents unnecessary errors from being made, also the savings gained because of shorter request processing and client servicing time arising from an integrated IT system. With an interconnected digital platform, there is full visibility of information and seamless information flow. This increases process transparency, boosts service availability, and promotes customer confidence. The benefits and return on investment need to be carefully worked out by the change management team together with the chief financial officer and be endorsed by executive management. Articulating the relevant benefits at this stage is crucial as it serves to align the executive management team toward a common goal.

Once the digital transformation strategy and vision for change have been endorsed by executive management, it should be cascaded to middle management and the rank and file. Then, projects teams with carefully selected candidates could be formed to execute the activities, track performance, and provide regular feedback to the sponsors. Ongoing alignment and engagement activities for the various key stakeholders should be arranged. In addition, the organization should evaluate the success of implementation using employee and customer satisfaction surveys. With proper evaluation, the organization would be able to ascertain the effectiveness of the digital transformation effort in achieving a positive outcome or otherwise.

MANAGING KEY STAKEHOLDERS

Change management involves effectively balancing the driving and restraining forces to change. If groups or individuals perceive that the change will be a threat to their interest, resistance will arise. Different change management strategies would have to be tailored for the various groups in the organization. A lot of attention is needed to address employee concerns related to the question, 'What's in it for me?' Executive and middle management must address any job-related fears, discuss the issues arising, and help employees transition into the new ways of working. The fear of job loss is a real problem for many employees. Thus, steps must be taken to help employees understand how the change will affect their jobs, also the types of assistance such as training and development workshops and career transition programs that are available. Over time, a higher level of trust would be established, leading to lower levels of resistance. With a structured and well-thought-through process, affected parties will have a better understanding of the new objectives and be able to embrace a new digital work environment.

In most organizational hierarchies, there are three clear segments or levels of employees. They are executive management, middle management, and the rank and file. Executive management occupies the highest level and consists of C-suite officers, such as the chief executive officer, chief operating officer, chief financial officer, chief information officers, and vice-presidents of business units. They oversee the entire organization and are responsible for the strategic direction of the business. Middle management usually takes on the roles of department heads and line managers. They supervise sub-units of the organization. The rank and file represents most of the workforce in the organization. They could either be from a business or support function dealing with day-to-day operations or administrative work. While these employees represent three distinct segments within the organization, they are part of an ecosystem. Their work is inter-related, and their relationships are inter-dependent. Strong teamwork and co-operation are needed among the various levels for organizational success. The success of a digital transformation effort depends heavily on obtaining buy-in across all segments of the organization. Very often, it takes more time to convince the organization that it should change its ways of doing things than to build the actual digital platform itself. It requires a lot of time and signification effort. However, such activities are necessary to build lasting change in the organization. Thus, change management activities must take into consideration all the segments since everyone plays a role in the digital transformation journey.

Executive management is a major group of stakeholders. They set the organization's direction and are involved in all the key decisions which affect the long-term survival of the organization. These C-suite executives and unit heads very often play the roles of executive sponsors and project owners. As digital transformation efforts can be quite disruptive to existing operations, they provide the much-needed leadership and commitment. Executive management must coordinate and collaborate with the rest of the organization to address the challenges and not leave it to their subordinates to manage the major issues. They need to invest their time and effort to craft key messages, make announcements at major forums, and conduct questions and answers sessions that are targeted at different segments of the organization. Without their buy-in and support, it is impossible to pursue any projects meaningfully. If they are not committed to the cause, the rest of the organization would have even less incentives to do so. Many organizations understand that simply appointing an uncommitted senior executive as point person to manage digital transformation is ineffective. Thus, executive management support is a critical success factor in change management. It is important to secure executive management buy-in early.

The executive management team has greater exposure to the strategic issues faced by the organization. In general, they are more keenly aware of the threats and the rationale for change. However, there are many factors that may influence executive management's attitude toward digital transformation, for example, conflicting organizational priorities. Resistance from the group may be due to the need to maintain stability despite market disturbances. The executive management may have to ensure that it is business as usual so that the organization can ride through difficult times. Consequently, the topmost priority may be to preserve the status quo rather than driving change which will bring about even more uncertainties. There could also be pressures from shareholders to meet short-term financial targets since most digital transformations take a few years to achieve any results. These factors will divert executive management attention away from digital transformation initiatives.

Thus, prior to implementation, the executive management team needs to know why it is necessary and crucial for the organization to embark on a digital transformation journey and buy-in to the idea. They need to show acceptance for doing digital transformation initiatives. Also, to demonstrate the willingness to actively support and participate in all the related activities. It is vital to align the leadership and secure their commitment early in the digital transformation project. Thus, meetings with executive management should be conducted to prepare the organization for change. The main purpose is to align management expectations and identify issues regarding the digital transformation journey. Their inputs such as organizational change readiness, change priorities, and gaps should be incorporated into the change management plan. Executive management must acknowledge the need for a change, and they must reach a consensus on the extent of change that they are willing to support.

Excellent visionary leadership and executive sponsorship are essential for a successful digital transformation program (Leinwand & Rotering, 2017). They must lead and build a culture that embraces change through digital transformation, to encourage the organization to experiment new ideas and accept that failures are an essential part of success. Executive management must be steadfast in championing the vision and maintaining an open line of communication across the organization. They must take into consideration the organization's existing culture, workplace factions, and office politics. External consultants can be employed to advise executive management on how to inculcate digital mindsets in the organization and translate them into behaviors and actions. There are benefits to bringing in external expertise to guide the development of a digital culture transformation program. They can augment existing organizational development capabilities and help to reduce uncertainties during implementation. However, executive management must take ownership to advocate these values and not leave it to the external consultants to drive the program on their behalf.

Assuming that there is already a strong buy-in from the executive management team, the next target group will be the middle management. As a group, the middle management has a much larger number of headcounts and is spread widely across the organization. They usually assume the roles of department heads and line managers and are responsible for implementing the strategies and policies. Middle management functions as a conduit between executive management and the employees on the ground. In fact, the executive management team relies on middle management to implement the plans and changes. Therefore, executive management should carefully plan on how to engage middle management and cascade the intention to them. A high level of commitment from the middle management is essential for digital transformation to be successful.

Middle management is 'sandwiched' between executive management and the rank and file. Most of their time could be spent 'fire-fighting' routine matters instead of planning for future developments. They face many challenges executing their daily tasks. For example, while middle managers are usually in the front line dealing with day-to-day operational issues and have a thorough understanding of customer problems, they lack the real power to make strategic decisions. They may be owners of business processes, but middle managers are not permitted to make changes beyond the tactical level. Their concerns are mainly to 'do things right' by following standard procedures and avoiding mistakes. Very often, they are required to refer to executive management for major decision-making. A major challenge facing middle managers is in balancing operational demands and the additional workload brought about by digital transformation. An organization embarking on a digital transformation program means extra responsibilities and heavier workload that are over and above the daily job requirements. Furthermore, they are expected to assimilate the digital technologies identified into the business activities. They may also believe that the existing processes are working well, and no major improvements are necessary. Along the way, they need to motivate and educate the rank and file to adopt the new digital technologies and processes. Thus, it is not uncommon that there will be strong resistance to change in middle management because a great deal of effort is required from them to move away from the status quo. They may not be fully convinced about the benefits of digital transformation.

Due to the diverse nature of the middle-management segment, it is a good practice to identify a core group of middle managers to obtain their buy-in first before reaching out to the rest. This group of high-potential managers can help to ignite passion among their peers. They can assist to disseminate relevant information about the digital transformation initiative and garner more support with the help of executive management.

In addition, to accelerate the widespread adoption of digital transformation practices, executive management can empower middle managers by giving them more authority over various business and support functions, and projects. Doing so will help middle management to develop a stronger sense of ownership and control over what they do, thereby, improving performance. Boosting the competencies of middle managers is another important area. Many key technical skills such as data analytics, artificial intelligence, and cybersecurity are needed for digital transformation. Besides these 'hard skills', middle managers require 'soft skills' training in problem-solving, empathy, and communication among others to succeed. A well-trained middle manager is not only able to perform specific tasks better but will be more confident to explore new areas and opportunities. They will be better equipped to manage and educate the rank and file. It is also important to engage the middle management in other ways. To emphasize the urgency for change, a series of workshops can be conducted for middle management to highlight the digital vision and action plans. Work groups can also be formed to study the current problems and recommend digital transformation projects to improve performance. Through middle management's involvement in the discussion of key organizational issues, they will understand first-hand the difficulties faced. Their participation in proposing solutions will also help to strengthen their ownership in digital transformation projects. The key outcome is to ensure that middle management understands the reasons and purpose for the digital transformation journey. Finally, executive management must listen to the problems surfaced by middle managers, collaborate with them to address the challenges upfront, and provide additional resources to support them to implement the changes.

The rank and file forms the bulk of the employees in the organization. They are responsible for the daily operations of the organization and are very familiar with existing processes and operational details. The rank and file deals with the customers directly and is in the best position to manage customer reactions and expectations. Securing their commitment to digital transformation will increase the probability of success for the initiative. However, as front liners, they may feel uncomfortable to utilize new digital technologies or change the existing workflow. Consequently, they may not respond well to digital transformation activities. Like the other stakeholder groups, proper communication and training can help to overcome their resistance to change. Many of the doubts and concerns can be addressed by executive management directly or through middle management.

The vision and high-level goals must be contextualized for the rank-and-file segment. The key gains of digital transformation should be translated to the individual level so that they understand that change is necessary and will benefit them. If the organization can communicate the value of a digital transformation initiative well, the rank and file should experience lesser doubts over time. The organization should also identify the different profiles of employees based on their readiness for change. These sub-groups could be those who are enthusiastic about change, those who conform to corporate directions, and those who have genuine work concerns. The organization can then design specific interventions to provide information to address their worries or training to prepare them for the digital transformation journey. Very often, the rank and file take the cue from their managers and supervisors. If the organization's direction is to embark on a new digital transformation initiative, the rank and file will usually follow if their superiors take the lead.

MANAGING COMMUNICATION

Robust communication is another critical success factor in change management (Lauer, 2021). Customized messages should be developed and shared with different segments of the organization. Well-crafted messages help to improve stakeholder buy-in. Some of these messages could include the vision and case for change for digital transformation. In addition, the communication messages should also highlight how the digital technologies are applied in the actual work settings and benefits to be gained. For example, the purpose of introducing robotic process project is to automate the labor-intensive transportation of inventory products, and the main benefits are increased efficiency and cost savings.

One approach in communicating change is to dispel any untruths arising from misinformation or lack of information. Employees should be provided with accurate information, even if it is negative news. All too often an organization assumes that communication simply means notifying the users through emails and keeping them informed of the project status. To make matters worse, many of these messages are frequently worded in a matter-of-fact tone. The outcome is that the message is more informational than inspirational. Consequently, employees may end up feeling unhappy because their concerns have not been fully addressed causing much resentment. It is a good practice to communicate with the stakeholders early in the project life cycle before any change is about to be implemented. There is an advantage in involving stakeholders sooner than later. This is because people need time to assimilate and internalize new information before they would act on them. For example, in a digital transformation project, the organization could identify the key users and involve them earlier in the gathering of system requirements. By engaging and communicating with the relevant parties early in the change process, the employees would have more time to consider both the present and future IT system requirements, resolve any outstanding issues with the developers, and generate stronger buy-in even before the IT system is developed. As part of continuous communication, they should also be actively involved in the design, development, and testing phases.

No digital transformation initiative could succeed without good communication across the whole organization. However, communicating to different levels of the organization, namely executive management, middle management, and rank and file could be challenging. This is because teams and individuals have different informational needs. A comprehensive communication strategy would be useful to engage different segments of the organization. The main goals of a communication management plan are to create awareness regarding the value of change and promote enthusiasm in the workplace in accepting change. Good communication would help to reduce resistance from the affected parties (Peacock, 2017). The communication plan should include details such as what information people would need, when this information would be made available, and who is responsible to release the information.

Activities such as project launches, townhalls, seminars, workshops, and training sessions should be planned to promote active participation and interactions among the players. Sometimes, it may be necessary to formally launch a digital transformation initiative to signify its importance to the organization. The executive sponsor could announce the launch and conduct a briefing prior to the commencement of the project. The agenda could cover the business case for the digital transformation, benefits to be reaped, specific activities, and the available resources in greater detail. Subsequently, dialogues, road shows, and feedback sessions could be organized for employees to clarify issues and suggest improvements. These events would also serve as communication channels to highlight key messages related to the digital transformation initiative. In highlighting the messages, the organization could provide the employees with an understanding of what is going on and why specific actions are being taken. This would help them to stay informed and engaged as digital transformation progresses. In addition, every effort should be made to keep communication lines open because resistance would grow to unmanageable levels when employees lose faith and trust in the organization. Finally, feedback mechanisms to assess the impact of messages and channels such as internal newsletters, web pages, staff forums, and corporate intranet should be instituted.

The organization must also communicate with its external stakeholders. External stakeholders include business partners, suppliers, government, and interest groups. Digital transformation may involve policies changes that require external parties' acceptance of new business propositions. To secure active participation from these stakeholders, the organization should prepare a set of viable business propositions specifically for them. This may involve crafting a narrative around the advantages of digital transformation for the partner ecosystem and industry. In addition, the benefits would have to be translated into dollar value to convince the partners that this is much to gain in this initiative. Industry forums and dialogue sessions could be organized to engage these interested parties. This should strengthen the value proposition for all the parties involved and boost the level of support and participation.

MANAGING COMPETENCIES

Training management is another important element of change management. The lack of proper training contributes significantly to employee resistance because of the fear associated with the inability to cope with new job requirements (Zukof, 2021). Many employees may be willing to change but lack the necessary knowledge and skills to perform the new activities required. When this happens, resistance to digital transformation grows. To overcome such obstacles, training could be provided to re-skill, up-skill, or cross-skill the affected employees. A systematic and structured training program would serve to accelerate the rate of adoption of digital technologies. It is also important to consider education and training programs for the different segments of the organization. Very often, besides the rank and file, members of the executive or middle management may also need some form of IT and soft skills training.

In training and development, there are some key factors that should be noted at the onset. Firstly, employees need to understand that training and development are important and would help them perform their jobs better. Consequently, employees must take any training provided seriously because the organization is in effect investing in their future. Secondly, the curriculum should be specially designed and targeted at specific employee segments depending on organization and training needs. The training plan and format for middle management would be quite different for those in the rank and file. For example, to create greater awareness among executive and middle management, learning journeys and expert seminars featuring IT-enabled industry trends and successful digital transformation use cases could be regularly introduced to help them keep abreast of new developments. Thirdly, the training agenda should be broad-based and cover both the 'why' and 'how'. The training should not only be just focusing on the functionalities and features of the new IT system. It should be scenario-based, that is, the training should cover how the new IT system is used in a particular situation. Finally, the application of new knowledge and skills to the actual working environment is a crucial consideration for real change to happen. Therefore, the training should be mapped to the actual work situations faced by the employees. When this happens, employees would be better equipped with the necessary skills to confidently perform new activities and tasks.

In the design and delivery of training, the trainers should consider areas such as learners' profile, adult learning theories, instructional strategies, and assessment. The learners' profile is an important aspect of training design and delivery. To prepare for a training course, the trainer needs to understand the class composition and representation to design an effective curriculum. To obtain this information, the trainers would have to discuss the training objectives and key learning outcomes with the human resource unit and other relevant stakeholders. A typical training class could consist of professionals, managers, and executives (PMEs) with an equal gender representation. The participants may have at least two to six years of relevant work experience. They could be mostly local employees. Further profiling could include their language proficiency and whether they hold formal education qualifications. The trainer would have to factor in these demographics in the training design and delivery. Adult learning theories and principles are important because they form the basis for trainers to support adults in the learning process. Some of the learning theories include critical thinking, self-directed learning, and transformative learning.

Adult participants generally prefer a more collaborative environment and utilize a problem-based approach to learning. Very often, although the participants may be from the same organization, they may not be familiar with one another. The trainers would have to incorporate group learning activities so that the participants can get to know each other better and learn from one another as part of the training. Specific instructional strategies could be applied to enhance the acquisition and internalization of knowledge for the participants. It is a 'different strokes for different folks' approach to cater to the different learning needs of individuals. For example, an instructional strategy that can be used to help critical learners assimilate information better is to include probing questions so that they can start to explore the underlying assumptions to certain issues. Attention should be focused on helping participants progress from the most basic level of data recall to higher level of analysis where they can see patterns and identify components. Participants who are new to a topic may be at a 'receive level' where they can only ask basic questions. The challenge would then be to raise the participants' ability to the 'value level' where they can discuss relevant issues more in-depth. To take into consideration the different learning styles, a variety of activities such as short presentations, mini-lectures, video case studies, and breakout discussions could be introduced to enhance training. To tap on the overall expertise of the class, individuals could be invited to share their experiences and reflections after each short presentation by the trainer. Video case studies of real companies undergoing digital transformation could be used to ensure that the lesson focuses on real-life problem-solving. One technique to promote retention of knowledge among the participants is through elaboration. At the debrief after a breakout discussion, questions could be posed to the participants to develop or present an idea in further detail. Participants could also be encouraged to suggest implications to expand on the knowledge of what they have already learned. It is important to recognize that each participant is a unique individual with different learning needs and styles. Thus, the trainers must always keep an open mind and look out for opportunities to introduce new techniques to help participants acquire and assimilate knowledge.

Assessment is an essential component of training as it is a process which gathers evidence to demonstrate that the intended learning outcomes have been achieved. It is an indication that the participants have attained a certain level of competency as a result of the training provided. Consequently, the confirmation of assessment requirements, methods, and tools with the relevant stakeholders is an important validation activity to ensure that the training process accurately evaluates the competencies that meet the needs of the organization. Providing clear and constructive feedback to the participant is a crucial step in training. The participant should be made aware of the areas in which he or she has done well and areas where there could be improvements.

Post-training information should be collected and analyzed on the efficiency and effectiveness of the instruction. Training evaluations should be conducted for three groups of people. The first group is the participants. Data on how participants feel about the actual training after the class should be collated to assess whether the training received is adequate for the new roles. The second group is the trainers. A debrief by the trainers on what they think were the topics participants find most difficult could help improve the syllabus for subsequent batches. Finally, training evaluation should also be conducted for the supervisors of the participants. Learning occurs when employees could apply the knowledge and skills acquired during training to actual work situations. The feedback of the supervisors is an indication on training effectiveness on whether the participants could apply the knowledge and skills learned in the actual working environment.

SUSTAINING CHANGE

Digital transformation is about change. This change is related to the way people think and act. For example, it would be very difficult to adopt a new business model if employees have a 'legacy mindset', that is, 'sticking to the old ways of doing things'. Thus, the organization must strive to inculcate an open culture that questions legacy practices and outdated processes. This can only be achieved when people feel that it is safe to experiment with new ideas, make mistakes, and improve on their work. Consequently, the organization should engage the employees early to prepare them for change. Organizations can introduce interventions that encourage people to embrace change and technology. Doing so involves modifying the overall work culture and individual mindsets regarding digital transformation. Executive management can create a conductive culture where people feel and are comfortable to experiment with new innovations. As far as possible, employees should be encouraged to view themselves as part of a larger system and take ownership to achieve the corporate goals above and beyond their own line and support duties. Some interventions that could help sustain change include creating incentives, redesigning job roles, and aligning workplace behaviors to core values.

The organization could consider designing incentives to recognize employees who exhibit certain desired workplace behaviors, for example, teamwork. Creating incentives help to address employee commitment issues, such as perceived fairness related to workplace contributions (Harrington, 2018). More importantly, these incentives promote the types of behaviors which the organization would like to be cultivated over the longer term. Incentives could either be monetary based such as bonuses, increments, and allowances or non-monetary based such as time-offs and mentoring programs. They could be either individual or team-based and for the short-term or the long-term. Regardless of the form, the idea of having incentives is to recognize employee contribution and reinforce the types of behaviors that are favorable to the digital transformation effort. For example, the implementors and change agents of the digital transformation initiative perform a key role in driving the major project activities and assisting other employees during the transition. In the process, they need to create a supportive work environment for change and motivate their colleagues whenever problems arise (Davis, 2017). Thus, it is important to provide incentives for this group of employees to drive change. In fact, all the teams and individuals who are directly involved in digital transformation should be formally recognized. To accelerate the rate of acceptance, other employees who embrace the new digital transformation initiative should also be identified and rewarded. The most direct way is to link employee contribution to their annual performance appraisal as a key result area.

Organizational work processes and job roles dictate the logical flow of work activities and play a significant part in shaping employee behaviors. If the processes are optimized, the organization would tend to be more agile and responsive to customer needs. Unfortunately, many organizations may still have many cumbersome and tedious work processes in place due to legacy issues. One approach in sustaining change is through job redesign. Job redesign serves to remodel work tasks and responsibilities to make the job more interesting. In addition, it also provides growth opportunities, increased responsibilities, and advancement for the employees. A well-designed job role helps to direct and channel employee efforts toward digital transformation and other related activities. Since the job description stipulates that the employee must act in a certain way on a regular basis, it would make it much easier for the employee to perform the expected tasks over the long run.

Organizational culture arises from the set of core values and beliefs held by a group of people working together. This culture is often manifested through observable employee behaviors. Thus, an organization embarking on a digital transformation journey could influence employee behaviors that are conducive to change through core values alignment. Values alignment involves identifying the set of core values which the organization stands for and translating them into observable desirable behaviors that employees are expected to demonstrate at the workplace. For example, if one of the core values championed by the organization is teamwork, an observable desirable behavior could be the employee's willingness to share resources when needed. Another observable behavior could be that the employee provides help when requested. Essentially, values alignment seeks to create a list of observable behaviors based on the organization's core values so that employees could learn to behave in a certain way. Coupled with appropriate positive reinforcement interventions such as incentives, permanent modifications to employee behaviors could be achieved to sustain change.

CASE ILLUSTRATION

Carousell is an online classifieds marketplace that makes selling and buying easy. The Singapore company is one of the world's largest and fastest-growing classifieds and serves tens of millions of customers across Southeast Asia and beyond. Its direction is to inspire people to start selling and buying from one another. The workplace culture emphasizes solving problems at scale with technology, connecting with the community, being resourceful, and staying humble (Carousell, n.d.). It is not an easy task to keep everyone moving forward in the company's direction as the company grows bigger. With the original team of three founders expanding to more than 500 full-time employees in several countries, the staff sometimes may not be able to interact regularly, which leads to people having different ideas on the app's direction (Huang, 2018). The Carousell founders recognize the importance of aligning employees with the company's direction and contextualizing their work to this goal. Thus, an organization-wide weekly meeting called Family Friday is held to communicate important business happenings, project updates, and interesting topics for everyone.

SUMMARY

This chapter emphasizes the need for having a digitally ready workforce and equipping them with the necessary digital competencies for digital transformation. People make things happen, so it is vital to focus on the people side of change. True change can only happen when the organization understands the real reasons for change and is aligned to the goal. The organization needs to develop a robust change management plan to address all the people issues arising from digital transformation. A well-thought-out change management plan is useful in proactively managing stakeholder engagements, communication, and competency development throughout the digital transformation journey. The major change management activities include stakeholder management, communication management, and training management. Finally, to sustain change, the organization needs to design structures and processes that encourage people to embrace change. The focus should be on organizational culture development so that employees adopt the right mindsets for digital transformation. Some of the interventions include creating incentives, redesigning job roles, and aligning workplace behaviors to core values.

REFERENCES

Bashir, S., & Miyamoto, K. (2020). *Digital skills: Frameworks and programs.* International Bank for Reconstruction and Development, The World Bank. https://openknowledge.worldbank.org/bitstream/handle/10986/35080/Digital-Skills-Frameworks-and-Programs.pdf?sequence=1

Carousell. (n.d.). *Who we are.* https://careers.carousell.com/who-we-are/

Davis, B. (2017). *Mastering organizational change management.* J. Ross Publishing.

Harrington, H. J. (2018). *Innovative change management: Preparing your organization for the new innovative culture.* Productivity Press.

Hiatt, J. (2006). *ADKAR: A model for change in business, government, and our community.* Prosci Learning Center Publications.

Huang, E. (2018). Carousell co-founder Marcus Tan's grand vision for the mobile marketplace. *KrAsia*. https://kr-asia.com/carousell-co-founder-marcus-tans-grand-vision-for-the-mobile-marketplace

Kotter, J. P., Brown, T., Martin, R. L., & Rigby, D. K. (2021). *HBR's 10 must reads on change management*. Harvard Business Review Press.

Lauer, T. (2021). *Change management fundamentals and success factors* (1st ed.). Springer, Berlin, Heidelberg. https://doi.org/10.1007/978-3-662-62187-5

Leinwand, P., & Rotering, J. (2017). How to excel at both strategy and execution. *Harvard Business Review*. https://hbr.org/2017/11/how-to-excel-at-both-strategy-and-execution

Orduna, N. (2021). Success with the internet of things requires more than chasing the cool factor. *Harvard Business Review*. https://hbr.org/2021/03/why-robots-wont-steal-your-job

Peacock, M. J. (2017). *The human resource professional's guide to change management: practical tools and techniques to enact meaningful and lasting organizational change* (1st ed.). Business Expert Press.

Rosenbaum, D., More, E., & Steane, P. (2018). Planned organizational change management: Forward to the past? An exploratory literature review. *Journal of Organizational Change Management*, *31*(2), 286–303. https://doi.org/10.1108/JOCM-06-2015-0089

Sage-Gavin, E., Vazirani, M., & Hintermann, F. (2019). Getting your employees ready for work in the age of AI. *MIT Sloan Management Review*. https://sloanreview.mit.edu/article/getting-your-employees-ready-for-work-in-the-age-of-ai/

Strohmeier, S. (2020). Digital human resource management: A conceptual clarification. *German Journal of Human Resource Management*, *34*(3), 345–365. https://doi.org/10.1177/2397002220921131

Tang, K. N. (2019). *Leadership and change management* (1st ed.). Springer Singapore. https://doi.org/10.1007/978-981-13-8902-3

Zukof, K. (2021). *The hard and soft sides of change management*. Association for Talent Development.

4

Experimental Learning and Design Thinking

> Think of digital transformation less as a technology project to be finished than as a state of perpetual agility, always ready to evolve for whatever customers want next, and you'll be pointed down the right path.
>
> **Amit Zavery, Google**

LEARNING BY TRYING OUT NEW THINGS

The digital world is characterized by rapid technological changes and fierce competition. Constant and unpredictable changes in market conditions and customer preferences are a norm (Diderich, 2020). In a volatile, uncertain, complex, and ambiguous (VUCA) world, organizations are constantly challenged to develop more innovative products and services. However, organizations must avoid traditional and outdated business practices. It is imperative that the organizations actively promote creativity and innovation to stay ahead of the market curve. To manage uncertainties, an organization could adopt an experimental learning mindset to try out new ideas or methods and learn from the market. In general, experimental learning refers to learning through practice. The practice involves conducting experiments to validate assumptions about the customers. Through repeated experimentations and tests, products and services can be modified and refined over time. The organization would benefit from this gradual approach because the resources required and risks involved are significantly less. A well-designed experiment is a discovery process to better understand and explore customer needs, their behaviors, and their expectations.

DOI: 10.1201/9781003311393-5

Experiments could be used either to introduce new ideas or investigate a perplexing issue. These experimentations require careful and close observation of customer behaviors to derive key insights about their real challenges and needs. By systematically varying the conditions in a particular setting, new knowledge could be gained about customer actions and their experiences. These inputs could then be incorporated in the next version of product and service design. Many organizations commit a common error of embracing an idea without testing the assumptions behind the concept (Lewrick et al., 2018). Assumptions are deeply held and accepted 'truths' about something. In all fields of studies, beliefs and notions are developed over time and added to a common body of knowledge. These firmly held ideas are thought to be 'true' and receive wide acceptance. To gain completely new insights, there is a need to test these assumptions by asking questions such as 'What if the assumption is wrong?' Challenging fundamental assumptions is a useful technique to achieve breakthrough results. The reason is that existing products and services are all designed and developed based on some preconceived notions. Once these notions change, the new designs which follow would essentially be very different from the initial ones. The testing of assumptions is an iterative process, and there is a lot of trial and error involved to determine what works and what does not. Nonetheless, in a VUCA world, these experiments and tests become even more crucial for organizations to better understand customer needs and wants.

In a 'phygital' world where customer interactions occur across a blend of physical and digital domains, there are plenty of opportunities for organizations to experiment with different approaches to engage and delight the customers. There are many new products and services that require trials and proof of concepts. To make these innovations work, organizations need to understand customer problems and deploy the appropriate technologies to overcome these challenges. Digital solutions are more about meeting the customer's real needs rather than deploying them just for the sake of technology. Many organizations have opted to set up innovation labs to promote digital transformation. Such facilities offer a destination for diverse stakeholders to co-create digital solutions to solve industry challenges. New ideas could be tested by design teams and the prototypes showcased to demonstrate their viability. In conjunction with these innovation labs, numerous hackathons are also organized to generate new business ideas which usually result in the development of a new app or service model. Essentially, these design sprint events attempt to bring together different groups of people to generate innovative ideas to solve real-world problems using digital technology. An extension to this approach for digital transformation is to identify entrepreneurs to take the innovative idea to the commercial stage through a startup. Startups are core to the digital transformation landscape because their innovations are generally representative of the shifts in the industry and the community. To support these startups, an initial seeding funding is usually provided to the teams with the best ideas to kickstart the digital business.

The internet has provided a highly networked environment that makes online experimentation easy to deploy. Many digital organizations have set up A/B testing programs to evaluate customer behavior with tremendous speed and scale. Such tests are a means by which organizations can quickly learn about customers' responses to new products and services and make informed decisions about any new ideas. A/B testing is relatively easy to deploy online and has low implementation cost. In an A/B test, two groups of experiences are usually set up: 'A' is the control group representing the current mode of operations while 'B' is the experimental group to be tested with modifications or improvements in the new way. These improvements could be a new feature, new layout, or new business rule. Customers are randomly assigned to the groups and the matrices are compared. With these results, the organization could identify the best touchpoint design and offerings for the customers. In fact, organizations could use online A/B tests to quickly learn and optimize any aspect of the business. By pushing new ideas out to a small, randomly selected group of customers and obtaining their feedback, enhancement can be made before these innovations are released to the entire customer base. The internet has made large-scale experimentation possible. Through the revelation of large numbers of customers' reactions to changes, organizations could gauge the effect of introducing new products and services. Thus, experimentation is useful because it builds customer knowledge by understanding their preferences. Eventually, the empirical data collected allows organizations to spot opportunities and guide business decisions.

UNDERSTANDING USER BEHAVIORS

Human-centered design is especially important in a 'phygital' world. Technology solutions that are developed must be personalized and take into consideration user preferences and pain points (Penzenstadler, 2020). Much attention should be focused on managing intangibles such as customer expectations, experience, and emotions. To be human-centered means putting people rather than other factors such as the organization or industry as the main consideration in the solution design. The development of a digital solution needs to adopt a more human-centered approach to improve user experience. Many applications are designed for the 'perfect user'. However, humans are prone to making mistakes and are not necessarily rational and fact-based all the time. Therefore, the design of digital platforms and applications must consider the emotional and experiential aspects of the users. This is where having an empathetic mindset is crucial in human-centered design where relationships is an important factor (Devecchi & Guerrini, 2017). It is the ability to put oneself in the shoes of others and derive insights to solve real-life problems.

One technique which emphasizes a human-centered approach to solve problems is design thinking. Design thinking seeks to recognize challenges from a user perspective to create innovative solutions (Brown et al., 2020). It helps organizations to stay focused on the human aspect and their needs. Through an iterative process of rapid prototyping and testing with the users, the problems are constantly being reframed and the solutions refined (Camacho, 2016). Design thinking is fundamentally about understanding people and creating solutions that they would use to solve problems. The goal is to understand the customers, identify their needs, define the desired outcomes, and design a great experience for product and service delivery. To better understand people and cultural systems, organizations need to develop insights into the relationships between the contexts and social processes of the customers (Whitehead, 2004). This falls within the field of ethnography. The study of ethnography seeks to know people from their point of view through empathy. It looks at human interactions with the world around them and the relationships that create 'meaning'. This helps the organization to make sense of a situation faced by the customer. Ethnography relies heavily on fieldwork and personal experience to identify peculiarities in human customs and habits. Some ethnographic research techniques include open-ended interviews, participant observation, and discourse analysis. Open-ended interviews do not have a predetermined set of answer choices so that interviewees respond to the questions in their own words. Participant observation seeks to learn about people performing activities under a natural setting. Discourse analysis attempts to study the 'meanings' from written and vocal records. These qualitative methods complement quantitative studies such as sampling and hypotheses testing. Quantitative methods are best applied when reliability and validity conditions are well-established. The cause-and-effect results produced are generally more convincing so that targeted remedial actions can be taken.

Customer science is an emerging field of study to better understand user experience in a customer journey. For example, when a customer has difficulties in a particular activity, what should be the remedy, and how long should the response time be. The entire practice is about making changes to improve customer experience based on the story which the collected data provides. It integrates behavioral science, data, and artificial intelligence to give a holistic view of the organization's engagement with the customers. A customer journey map is a good starting point to understand the customers' experiences with the organization's different touchpoints. It could also be used to diagram the activities that customers go through to accomplish a goal such as purchasing items or requesting for information. By mapping the customer journey, the organization can identify all the common customer pain points and discover any missed opportunities to interact with them at any stage. With the insights gained, the organization could provide further optimized and personalized customer experiences.

AN ITERATIVE PROCESS OF DISCOVERY

One well-established approach to design thinking consists of five stages: empathize, define, ideate, prototype, and test (Plattner et al., 2018; Tu et al., 2018). Empathy is central to the whole design thinking practice. It allows one to connect with others in a meaningful way. To empathize involves adopting a mindset to understand user issues from their perspective. It is essential because it serves to provide insights into the key issues and challenges faced. By understanding why and the way others do things, solutions can be better designed to meet their needs. The knowledge gained from identifying customers' physical and emotional needs, and what is meaningful to them, is vital in product development. With an empathetic mindset, design thinkers become more aware of customer behavioral patterns and the barriers that the customers are facing (Stanford et al., 2017). They put themselves in the 'shoes of the customers' and see the situation from their perspective. By looking from the customer's point of view, the design thinkers would appreciate and learn more about their needs and wants. This deep appreciation of user psyche and their interactions with the environment would form the basis for creative solutions to be generated. When a product or service meets a specific need, customers would begin to rely on them and use them more frequently. On the other hand, if a product is developed without a good understanding of customer behavior and with a lack of empathy, it is unlikely that the product would enjoy much commercial success.

There are several ways such as direct observations and dialogues to find out about another person's point of view (Hasso Plattner Institute of Design at Stanford, 2010). The most straightforward method is through direct observation of the user in action. It is watching the person complete a set of activities in the actual environment and asking the person to articulate the thoughts that are happening while performing the tasks. What the customers do and how they interact with their surroundings provide clues about what they think and feel. The organization can learn a lot about customer behaviors in the context of their lives and infer about what they need in those situations. Through the physical expressions of their experiences, namely the actions and speech, key insights could be generated. Sometimes, such insights are derived from a disconnect between what the customer says and what he or she does, also when customers create work-around solutions to settle minor irritations or disruptions in their daily activities. In such situations, the customer may not even mention it during the interviews as they themselves may not have paid much attention to these solutions. For the organization, these customer insights are vital because they provide the direction to create innovative products and services to meet a hidden need. However, a common pitfall in observation is the tendency to filter out important information due to observer biasness. Thus, organizations must try to resist this natural inclination and always strive to see things 'with a fresh pair of eyes'.

Customer dialogues is another effective method to learn about customer needs and behaviors. Essentially, the technique involves having a conversation with the customer. Through repeated discussions with the customer, a tremendous amount of information about their beliefs and values which they hold can be discovered. Storytelling is an important skill that can be applied in customer dialogues. This method provides an avenue to verbally explain values and share experiences with others. Storytelling is useful because it offers the context in which conflicts, preferences, and emotions experienced can be vividly communicated. Very often, the deeply held beliefs and values found in the stories are not obvious to the customers themselves. In creating a conversation, start by asking the customer the reason for trying to solve a particular problem. Then, let the customer share their stories from a list of open-ended questions and allow for any deviations from the main topic, if necessary. Try to understand the motivations behind the need to close this gap such as how are they currently resolving the problem and whether they have tried other methods to improve the situation. The whole idea is to uncover the real pain points. Also, try to detect the underlying cause and effect of actions. Similarly, avoid the pitfall of observer biases by putting away one's assumptions and paying close attention to what the customers say. Other tips include observing any special physical cues when they say something and take note of the language used and how they are phrased. Do not prompt them for answers or rush for responses and allow the customers to ponder and react naturally. Getting to the root cause of an issue is a critical first step of the exercise. The 'five whys' method is useful in this area. By asking 'why' repeatedly, the true cause of a problem could be uncovered. Finally, a useful tool to capture all the information is an empathy map with four quadrants about the customer: says, thinks, does, and feels. Essentially, it is a visual representation that summarizes the knowledge about a user's behaviors and attitudes and helps to identify the pains and gains.

Good designs are created based on a clear understanding of the customer's challenges and identifying creative ideas to address these problems. Thus, all the initial inputs will be very useful for hypotheses and prototypes development later. Once the information has been captured through preliminary observations and engagements with the customer, the organization may start to define the challenge. The definition stage is an attempt to frame an issue around the user, the actual needs, and goals to be achieved. In effect, it is about making sense of the information gathered and clarifying what should be the focus to solve the problem. These initial findings should be shared among the different teams in the organization to garner more ideas and solutions. A gallery walk activity will be useful in making sense of the vast amount of information gathered. In a gallery walk, all the information collected from the user is displayed on wall posters. The relevant stakeholders will do a walking tour and note down key points that they feel are important and relevant to the solution.

The key points are shared and discussed with others in the same session. Through this immersive exercise, further insights may be developed because those who did not participate in the collation of customer information earlier will get a chance to offer their views. Another advantage of using this approach is that it avoids the problem of observer bias because the collected information is presented to a new team. At the end of the gallery walk, the organization should incorporate all the different perspectives and build a value proposition that will resonate with the customers.

Problem definition is the step which helps to breakdown 'wicked problems' into smaller parts so that solutions can be more easily identified. A 'wicked problem' is a complex challenge with many dependencies and stakeholders involved. While the organization may have a general idea of the problem, much effort is required in scoping the issues correctly through requirements gathering. The goal is to craft an actionable problem statement based on a synthesis of the organization's understanding of the customer and problem faced. A well-defined and scoped challenge would accurately describe the problem and provide guidance to the designers in the subsequent evaluation of ideas. These problem statements may take the form of 'how might we …?' The way an organization defines the problem would to a great extent determine the level of innovation at the ideation stage. A narrowly and poorly defined challenge would limit the number of options explored and would not likely inspire one to come out with many creative ideas.

With the challenge defined, the next step is to ideate or generate as many ideas as possible to solve the problem. This requires divergent thinking to explore many possible solutions. Thus, the goal of ideation is to cast the net wide and look at the widest possible range of suggestions to choose from. The focus is on the quantity and less on the quality of ideas. The best idea can be determined at a later stage from user testing and customer feedback. Brainstorming is the most common technique used to generate many new ideas. Essentially, the organization states the problem statement, sets a time limit, and allows anyone to come up with as many ideas as possible during a workshop. Some important ground rules to take note of are to refrain from criticizing or judging any idea at this stage and to capture all the ideas even if they appear to be weird and wacky. The use of metaphors can help to spawn new ideas. The choice of the metaphor can be randomly generated. The purpose of the exercise is to associate key features of the metaphor and try to apply them to the business problems to derive learning points, and hopefully, new ideas to solve the challenge. Metaphors help to stimulate the right brain hemisphere deals primarily with pictures and stories. It could more easily make cross associations based on common characteristics of a metaphor. Another suggestion to produce ideas is to look across industries to find similarities to solve common problems. Looking beyond existing industry boundaries can help the organization discover creative ways or approaches that can be applied in the current context. Design thinking is a highly collaborative endeavor. It helps when there are inputs arising from diverse views and multiple perspectives. Through team interactions and group synergies, many creative solutions to the problem statement can be formulated. Thus, once these ideas have been collated, the next activity is to go beyond the obvious suggestions and explore possibilities through the collective perspectives of the organization.

Systems thinking is a useful practice to connect ideas to present an overview of the situation (Beckman, 2020). This tool allows organizations to better understand the 'big picture' and the main variables or issues that are causing the problems. Systems thinking serves to connect the dots and facilitates the building of an ecosystem to tackle wicked problems involving various stakeholders. It is a way of thinking for organizations to learn and adapt in a fast-changing environment. A system exists to accomplish a purpose and requires all its parts to accomplish this. The purpose can only be accomplished in balance with all the system parts. In a system, there are interrelated and interdependent parts or subsystems. An imbalance in the subsystem diminishes the overall system's ability to accomplish its activities. Systems thinking allows the organization to consider how the different parts interrelate and work as a whole. In the digital world, developing digital platforms and coopetition strategies among market players is a common strategy. Systems thinking is one approach that can address such issues more holistically. The organization would benefit from using a systems thinking approach as part of design thinking to understand how problems are interrelated.

The prototype stage offers another chance for direct conversations with the customer (Stackowiak & Kelly, 2020). In prototyping, the organization would normally build a preliminary model to test the concept. The main purpose is to create something which allows the user to interact with to collect feedback for further refinement. The prototype is the initial sample to be iterated before arriving at the final solution. Therefore, the prototype should be simple to make, and the materials used can be obtained easily. To build a prototype, start with items that are readily available at home or from the office. Focus on the hypotheses that the organization wishes to test with the customer. Break the large problem down into smaller and testable features or areas. Imbued it with the key features of the concept that the customer will need to solve the problem. Keep the prototype simple, cheap, and ready to be discarded after testing. The main point is to commit as few resources as possible at this stage. Even if the prototype fails, it will be at a low cost. Thus, low-fidelity prototypes are preferred. Low-fidelity prototypes are often paper-based models that do not allow much user interaction. These prototypes may be a storyboard, cardboard model, a role-playing activity, or a wireframe. A storyboard is an illustration of how a user would interact with the solution under various scenarios. A cardboard model could be a new gadget to be launched while a roleplay activity acts out a character for a new service. Finally, a wireframe shows the key interface components of mobile or web pages. When a design becomes more developed, high-fidelity prototypes that are more functional and interactive can be constructed.

When the preliminary model is ready to be tested, the customer would be brought in to try it out. This is an important stage for the organization to listen attentively and solicit feedback from the users. It is an opportunity to learn more about the solution and the user. The process is a validation of the proposed solution by the customers by means of usability testing. There are some points that should be observed when a test is conducted. Firstly, when the prototype is shown to the user, the testers should avoid trying to explain too much about its features beyond those instructions that are necessary for the user to handle it. Secondly, watch how the user interacts with the solution and record these observations without giving any feedback. Then, ask the user about the overall experience when trying out the prototype. A common mistake committed by the organization is to become 'defensive' over the solution and dismisses subtle cues from the users. Therefore, a key point to note is to remember that all the feedback should not be downplayed since the user is in the best position to know if the solution works. Finally, do remember to find out the underlying reasons why the customers like or dislike about the prototype. Once testing is completed, the user inputs are analyzed. It is very common that the organization would have to revisit the initial design thinking stages to refine the problem statement, generate more ideas, and create new prototypes for testing. In fact, 'failures' should be viewed favorably as a way for the organization to learn about how to enhance the product or service.

Although the five stages are presented in a linear manner, in practice, they are non-linear and iterative in nature. Design thinking should not be viewed as a structured process. This is because design activities are normally 'messy' and involve moving back and forth between the various stages as the problem becomes clearer and the solutions are progressively refined. Iterations are fundamental to good designs. For this reason, the organization should not expect a design thinking initiative to follow a strict order of events, rather to rely on an iteration of the five main steps in various cycles. Generally, as the scope narrows from a broad concept to the refinement of nuanced details, the cycle is repeated. The design thinking process relies on both analytical and intuitive styles of thinking (Combelles et al., 2020). Finally, design thinking is a learn-by-doing practice and depends heavily on the collaboration between users, stakeholders, and designers. The users and stakeholders will have to work together to co-create the design and arrive at a win-win situation. It is a discovery process where mutual benefits need to be identified and explored to arrive at a sustainable solution. No party should be made worse off in the new design.

USER EXPERIENCE DESIGN

User experience design simply means creating the best experience of using a product or service. In the context of digital transformation, it is generally associated with mobile, web, and software applications. With advances in digital technology, many features and functionality can be easily added to an application. These elements will make the application more appealing to the customer. For example, the customer may be able to receive timely information and navigate the site with greater ease. It is more important to emphasize user experience in terms of how the customers feel when they use the product or service (Dong & Liu, 2017). It is about how various emotions are evoked when the customer utilizes the application. The connection between human users and computer-based products and services becomes the focus. Just like design thinking, user experience design also uses a human-centered approach to create designs with a great sensory experience for the customer. There are many techniques that are used in user research, for example, personas, usability testing, card sorting, and eye movement tracking. A persona is a fictional representation of the characteristics of the ideal user (Coorevits et al., 2016). It is intended to give a dependable indication of how a group of people engages with the organization's product or service. Usability testing entails observing users completing the tasks with a product. The test is used to detect the problems faced by the user when working with the product. Card sorting allows the user to discuss and prioritize features and functionality by arranging a set of index cards. Eye movement tracking reveals where the user is looking when using the application. The user's point of gaze or eye motion will expose the key aspects of the product which attract the attention of the user.

User experience can be influenced by various factors. These factors include whether the product or service is useful, usable, findable, credible, desirable, accessible, and valuable (Morville, 2004; Rosenfeld et al., 2015). Briefly, the product is useful if it serves a purpose. Usable means that the product can serve the user in an efficient and effective manner. Findable refers to the ease of locating the product. Credible is the level of trust in using the product. Desirable relates to the strong feelings of wanting a particular product. Accessibility is associated with how well the product can be reached by different user groups. Finally, valuable means that the product can provide benefits that are meaningful to the user. To be able to deliver a great user experience, the organization must pay careful attention to these factors to differentiate itself with the competitors. When interacting with a computer-based product, a few interface elements also need to be taken into consideration. They are words, visual representations, space, time, and behavior (Interaction Design Foundation, n.d.). Words are concerned with how text is depicted in the user interface. Visual representations cover items such as images and icons. Space deals with the physical aspect of the interface. Time relates mostly to media such as videos and sounds but can also mean time spent using the product. Behavior refers to the actual conduct in using the product including the emotions experienced.

CASE ILLUSTRATION

Bus Uncle is a made-in-Singapore chatbot that announces bus arrival timings through applications such as Facebook Messenger, Telegram, and Google Assistant (Teo, 2018). Besides informing commuters about the availability of bus services and waiting time, the chatbot also engages in small talk with the users. Occasionally, Bus Uncle makes new product recommendations in the local colloquial conversations. The project arose because of a need to receive timely bus arrival timings without having to repeatedly refresh an app for updates (Murthy, 2017). Thus, a prototype was developed which automatically reads out available bus arrival timings. Overall time, the chatbot included new features such as the ability to tell jokes to entertain bored commuters while waiting for buses to arrive at the designated bus stop. The chatbot also assumed the persona of a bus captain. By adopting a design thinking approach to understanding customer pain points, the development team gathered numerous feedbacks from customers, friends, and colleagues and made many iterations to enhance the prototype. The result is a likeable chatbot with a jester-like personality which speaks Singlish, an informal form of the English language. More importantly, the design of Bus Uncle solves a very basic need of making an otherwise dull and boring bus-waiting period to something more interesting and informative.

SUMMARY

This chapter shows an approach to develop innovative products and services to stay competitive in an uncertain market environment. Through experimentations, the organization learns by trying out new things. In developing digital solutions, one of the key considerations is to understand human behaviors and how technology can be applied to solve a real problem. The chapter describes a popular design thinking process which includes activities to empathize, define, ideate, prototype, and test. Having an empathetic attitude is a major attribute for design thinkers because it allows them to see a particular situation or issue from another's perspective. Through an iterative design thinking process, a problem is reframed, refined, and tested with the customers. User experience design emphasizes creating the best experience of using a product or service for customers. In the context of digital transformation, it is generally associated with mobile, web, and software applications. Common factors affecting user design such as accessibility and credibility are discussed.

REFERENCES

Beckman, S. L. (2020). To frame or reframe: where might design thinking research go next? *California Management Review, 62*(2), 144–162. https://doi.org/10.1177/000812 5620906620

Brown, T., Christensen, C. M., Nooyi, I., & Govindarajan, V. (2020). *HBR's 10 must reads on design thinking*. Harvard Business Review Press.

Camacho, M. (2016). David Kelley: From design to design thinking at Stanford and IDEO. *She Ji, 2*(1), 88–101. https://doi.org/10.1016/j.sheji.2016.01.009

Combelles, A., Ebert, C., & Lucena, P. (2020). Design thinking. *IEEE Software, 37*(2), 21–24. https://doi.org/10.1109/MS.2019.2959328

Coorevits, L., Schuurman, D., Oelbrandt, K., & Logghe, S. (2016). Bringing personas to life: User experience design through interactive coupled open innovation. *Persona Studies, 2*(1), 97–114. https://doi.org/10.21153/ps2016vol2no1art534

Devecchi, A., & Guerrini, L. (2017). Empathy and design: A new perspective. *The Design Journal, 20*(sup1), S4357–S4364. https://doi.org/10.1080/14606925.2017.1352932

Diderich, C. (2020). *Design thinking for strategy innovating towards competitive advantage*. Springer International Publishing. https://doi.org/10.1007/978-3-030-25875-7

Dong, Y., & Liu, W. (2017). A research of multisensory user experience indicators in product usage scenarios under cognitive perspective. *International Journal on Interactive Design and Manufacturing, 11*(4), 751–759. https://doi.org/10.1007/s12008-016-0358-8

Hasso Plattner Institute of Design at Stanford. (2010). *An introduction to design thinking process guide*. Stanford University. https://web.stanford.edu/~mshanks/MichaelShanks/files/509554.pdf

Interaction Design Foundation. (n.d.). *What is interaction design?* https://www.interaction-design.org/literature/topics/interaction-design

Lewrick, M., Link, P., & Leifer, L. J. (2018). *The design thinking playbook: Mindful digital transformation of teams, products, services, businesses, and ecosystems*. John Wiley & Sons, Inc.

Morville, P. (2004). *User experience honeycomb*. Semantic Studios. http://semanticstudios.com/user_experience_design/

Murthy, A. (2017, February 17). *Why I created Bus Uncle*. Medium. https://medium.com/@abhilashmurthy/why-i-created-bus-uncle-40beb665c197

Penzenstadler, B. (2020). When does design help thinking, and when does design thinking help? *IEEE Software, 37*(2), 6–9. https://doi.org/10.1109/MS.2019.2958263

Plattner, H., Meinel, C., & Leifer, L. (2018). *Design thinking research - Making distinctions: Collaboration versus cooperation*. Springer. https://doi.org/10.1007/978-3-319-60967-6

Rosenfeld, L., Morville, P., & Arango, J. (2015). *Information architecture: For the web and beyond*. O'Reilly Media, Incorporated.

Stackowiak, R., & Kelly, T. (2020). *Design thinking in software and ai projects proving ideas through rapid prototyping*. Apress. https://doi.org/10.1007/978-1-4842-6153-8

Stanford, J., Siminoff, E. T., O'Neill, M., & Mailhot, J. (2017). *What is design thinking?* O'Reilly Media.

Teo, J. (2018, Sep 7). *It's not easy being Bus Uncle, Singapore's first AI influencer.* 8 Days. https://www.8days.sg/seeanddo/thingstodo/it-s-not-easy-being-bus-uncle-singapore-s-first-ai-influencer-10693070

Tu, J. C., Liu, L. X., & Wu, K. Y. (2018). Study on the learning effectiveness of Stanford design thinking in integrated design education. *Sustainability (Basel, Switzerland),* *10*(8), 2649. https://doi.org/10.3390/su10082649

Whitehead, T. L. (2004, March 27). *What is ethnography? Methodological, ontological, and epistemological attributes.* Cultural Ecology of Health and Change. https://static1.squarespace.com/static/542d69f6e4b0a8f6e9b48384/t/56495b19e4b0bfd3ce24605d/1447648025111/EpiOntAttrib.pdf

5

Digital Product Management

Don't be fooled by some of the digital transformation buzz out there, digital
transformation is a business discipline or company philosophy, not a project.

Katherine Kostereva, Creatio

NEW PRODUCTS DRIVE GROWTH

Product development is a key competitive advantage for organizations.
It is a means to drive business growth and stay ahead of competition
(Geissbauer et al., 2019). An organization's ability to rapidly create and
launch new products will determine whether it thrives or merely survives
in the marketplace. An organization must be highly responsive to ever-
changing market conditions and customer preferences. From an execution standpoint, the organization must continuously gather customer
feedback and very quickly translate these inputs into new feature releases.
For an organization to be able to achieve this capability, it requires a different approach to managing products.

In the context of digital transformation, the product would normally be
digital assets that are useful and provide value to the organization. Some of
the common digital assets include document files, images, and videos in
an electronic format. The digital products that are developed by the organization also fall within the digital assets category. These digital products
could be a single application or a suite of related software and information
technology (IT) services which collectively provide a digital solution to
meet a business need (Broadcom, 2020). For example, a customer relationship management application that is connected to a call center tele-
phony application and fully supported through hybrid cloud services.

DOI: 10.1201/9781003311393-6

A popular digital product is the digital platform which organizations develop as a base to integrate other applications and digital technologies. In recent years, many other types of digital assets such as cryptocurrencies and non-fungible tokens have been created and available in the market.

Traditionally, projects are established to create new products and services. The project management process is led by a project manager. To actively manage customer preferences and new digital products, a specialized role is required. It is the product manager role. The role is primarily customer focused, and the main activities are geared toward proactively anticipating changing customer needs (Gnanasambandam et al., 2017). A product manager plays a key role in an organization's digital transformation journey. There are many uncertainties and risks surrounding the product development process. Frequent and drastic changes to the product plan may be required. The product manager will have to adopt agile practices to execute the activities faster and develop a human-centered thinking mindset to better understand customer needs (Blosch et al., 2019).

A BOUNDARY SPANNING ROLE

As with most job roles and functions, the job description of a digital product manager can be mixed and varied. The specific requirements depend on several factors such as the needs of the organization and at which stage of the product's life cycle it is in. Nonetheless, there are a few key functions that are essential in executing the role of the digital product manager. Given its growing importance in recent years, many industry players and individuals have provided detailed descriptions of the nature of work and requirements for the product manager role (Cerri, 2019; Davenport, 2021; Jelen, 2019; ProductPlan, n.d.). Broadly, the product manager's job involves facilitating information flow from outside the organization to internal stakeholders. These boundary-spanning tasks are crucial in the digital world because customers are now interacting directly with the organization on a regularly basis whether through an application or otherwise. Thus, a role that constantly assesses the pulse of the industry and customers will be extremely beneficial to the organization.

The focus of a digital product manager is outward looking, with an emphasis on the market and customer needs (Cerri, 2019). He or she needs to have a good sensing of market trends and competitor positioning.

To reach a better understanding of the market, the digital product manager will have to conduct market research and competitor analysis to develop insights for the product strategy. As part of the function, the incumbent also takes on the position of a customer champion. The digital product manager will have to support the customers and speak on their behalf inside the organization. To ensure success, the digital product manager will have to actively solicit customer inputs through the organization's touchpoints, analyze the feedback, and propose actions to improve customer experience. Essentially, the digital product manager acts as a conduit to bring in insights from evolving market developments and shifting customer demands into the organization. He or she also serves as the voice of the customer to the organization's internal stakeholders, such as marketing, and works with them on outreach campaigns and activities (Jelen, 2019).

Another important function of a digital product manager involves setting the direction for the digital product. The product strategy encompasses crafting a narrative for the product, which includes the purpose, goals, objectives, and action plan (Layon, 2014). As part of the role, the digital product manager must strategize and prioritize the features for future product development. Conducting routine assessments of new and existing features forms a huge part of the work. He or she must continually raise questions and debate on the necessity for a particular feature for the customer vis-à-vis the needs of the organization. The digital product manager must maintain a features to-do list and ensure that backlogs are managed appropriately in response to changing customer demands and business objectives. The incumbent is also responsible for the product roadmap and is expected to share this knowledge with the rest of the organization (ProductPlan, n.d.), more importantly, to create more buy-in among the internal stakeholders for the digital product. To do so, the digital product manager would have to strengthen internal communication so that different levels of the organization support and participate more actively in the product development activities; separately, as an internal product champion, to ensure that sufficient resources such as manpower and budgets are allocated to the digital products; and, finally, to coordinate activities such as design, development, and testing to help optimize resources and shorten the digital product's time to market. To make things happen, the digital product manager would have to collaborate with designers, software developers, and members of IT operations to overcome business and technical constraints to reconcile with customer benefits.

The role of a digital product manager is closely tied to the life cycle of a product. From a market and customer perspective, the life cycle covers the development, introduction, growth, maturity, and decline of the digital product. The digital product manager is responsible for the digital product strategy including product vision, positioning, and differentiation, also the implementation activities related to the conceptualization, design, testing, production, and launch of the digital product. The digital product manager often employs a suite of techniques such as design thinking and DevOps to accomplish the various tasks. Design thinking is a method to create innovative solutions from a user perspective. DevOps is an approach that brings together software development (Dev) and IT operations (Ops) staff to ensure end-to-end service delivery. The digital product manager plays a boundary-spanning role in the management and development of digital products as part of the organization's digital transformation journey.

A WALKTHROUGH OF ACTIVITIES

An organization should put in place a product management process to better organize resources for the entire product life cycle. A well-defined set of product management roles, activities, and decision points will help the organization become effective in achieving its digital transformation goals. There are various key activities such as customer research, product design, and product marketing that a digital product manager is involved in (Kawamura et al., 2019; ProductPlan, n.d.). On a day-to-day basis, the digital product manager will be interacting with different internal stakeholders to manage the digital products, also to work externally with customers to improve their experience in using these products. To better visualize how a digital product manager can work collaboratively with business and support units, designers, software developers, and IT operations staff, a walkthrough of the activities for a hypothetical product management and development process will be briefly illustrated and explained next.

Beginning with a basic understanding of different customer behaviors and segments, a digital product manager will build on this knowledge by gathering more in-depth information about customer problems and needs from the organization's various touchpoints. The other types of collection methods used include focus groups and interviews. Once the initial hypotheses have been formed, the digital product manager will work with other team members from business, marketing, and design to generate ideas and propose an initial solution to solve the customers' problems. The digital product manager will also tap on available sources such as customer and supplier feedback, and staff suggestions. At this stage, the designers will be involved in creating low fidelity prototypes and experimenting different concepts and models. The team will produce a preliminary business case proposal that highlights the description of the proposed digital product, the benefits to be delivered to the customer, the options available, and some preliminary costings. The preliminary business case proposal will be presented to executive management for in-principle approval and further development of a more detailed report.

Once executive management gives the go-ahead for a detailed report, a digital product owner will be identified, and a multi-disciplinary team formed. Fundamentally, the digital product owner serves as an internal customer representative who will develop the digital product together with the team of designers, software developers, IT operations staff, and digital product manager. The whole team will collaborate to develop a detailed report which covers the product strategy, product roadmap, cost and benefit analysis, risk assessment, alternatives available, implementation timeline, and budget. An extensive cost and benefit analysis will be conducted to justify the digital initiative. The series of product planning activities will involve stakeholders from departments such as IT, finance, human resource, and legal. To ensure market viability for the digital product, there will be a thorough evaluation on all the crucial areas such as business goals, market analysis, product strategy, implementation roadmap, and financials prior to final approval by executive management.

Upon final approval, the earlier conceptualization and experimentation activities for the digital product are extended with the collection and analysis of more customer information to determine whether the intended benefits can be realized. At this stage, high-fidelity prototypes are built and tested with the customers to refine the features and functionalities. Key assumptions are challenged and verified to make sure that the digital product meets the underlying needs of the customer. The team will apply agile practices and design-thinking methods to help them figure out the preferred solution. The key requirements for the digital product are then established and the product direction finalized. With the involvement of the designers, software developers, and IT operations staff, all the specifications and improvements will be incorporated at the different stages of the software development life cycle. After various iterations, the digital product will be built and ready for launch. The digital product owner must then ensure that the digital product is tried out and proven to be usable. The digital product manager will then proceed to release digital product to the market, track its performance, solicit customer feedback, and continuously improve on it throughout the entire product life cycle.

CORE COMPETENCIES REQUIRED

Continuous incremental improvements made to a digital product in terms of features and functionalities ensure that it stays relevant in the market space and can keep up with changing customer preferences. The organization should be responsive and open to experimentations and iterations to continuously refine the digital product. To perform these activities well, the digital product manager must be equipped with some core competencies to overcome various common organizational challenges. For example, an organization may not have fully embraced the agile way and still be using traditional waterfall practices to develop digital projects. The rigidity of some waterfall method assumptions also restricts the extent of experimentation possible on the features and functionalities. Consequently, the level of responsiveness to customer demands may be compromised. Given this scenario, the digital product manager must have the requisite knowledge and skills to be able to strike a balance between applying the appropriate agile techniques which run in parallel with various linear and sequential product development activities. The digital product manager will have to be very careful in managing factors such as the speed of implementation and the risk arising from frequent requirement changes.

The role of a digital product manager spans organizational boundaries. Outside of the organization, he or she conducts market research to better understand customer experience and competitor strategies. This involves collecting, validating, and synthesizing a combination of primary, secondary, quantitative, and qualitative data. The knowledge and insights gained are translated into the product strategy and shared with different functional units within the organization. A common problem dealing with internal colleagues is the silo mentality. Some individuals and units may prefer to keep a distance and resent information requests from others. To overcome this difficulty, the digital product manager must have effective people managing skills to work with these stakeholders. In addition, have strong communication skills to clarify requirements with them and reduce unnecessary friction in the process. Thus, digital product managers must be both business savvy and technically competent to be able to discover customer needs and work collaboratively with various technical and functional teams to manage the entire product lifecycle.

In organizations where project-based methods are the dominant practice, some re-orientation is required to acquaint the stakeholders to adopt product management and development processes. Organizations which traditionally favor a project-centric approach to manage deliverables may find it difficult to transit into a product-centric model. The reason is that these approaches operate under a different set of philosophies, methodologies, and practices. In project management, the project manager is required to coordinate the activities of different stakeholders with well-defined deliverables to drive business success. With an established project management methodology and support provided by a project management office, the organization would perform many standard activities such as software implementations and marketing launches with the support of a project manager. In turn, the project manager would report to a group of key stakeholders, implement the fixed schedule, and ensure that the project is on time, on budget, and within scope. As a result of the differences in the way of working, some change management competencies will be required to help the organization adopt product management practices.

PROJECT MANAGEMENT REVISITED

Many organizations face pressures to deliver IT systems that are on time, on budget, and within scope. However, the hierarchical nature of organizations, with different levels of employees and a high degree of division of work, inadvertently slows down the IT delivery process. The vertical workflow in bureaucracies often results in bottlenecks and delays. To solve these problems, numerous organizations have adopted a project management approach to accelerate the achievement of business goals. Managing work as projects is a proven method that promotes cross-functional collaboration among different groups within the organization. The project management methodology promotes a flexible and efficient way of working on complex activities with many stakeholders. It is a tactical approach which assigns ownership and tasks to complete deliverables based on a planned timeline and allocated resources. In a project-centric setup, employees are required to work together both across functions and throughout the various levels of seniority. Consequently, project-related work tends to be more efficient and effective. Also, conflict between project management and unit function is minimized.

Most projects typically have a formal project management structure consisting of several key roles. During initiation, a project sponsor would commission and allocate resources for a project. The responsibility of the project sponsor is to set the direction, provide leadership, and make any final decisions on the project. A project owner who is the main beneficiary of the project deliverables is appointed. In addition, there would be a steering committee consisting of executive and middle management to review project issues and prioritize resources. The steering committee would conduct periodic reviews on the project activities and approve the deliverables. If there are changes to be made to the existing project plan, approval from the steering committee is required. In addition, the steering committee is also expected to resolve any conflicts arising from the different stakeholders. A project team led by a project manager is formed to manage the sequence of activities to deliver a product or outcome. The project team members are employees from different units who are assigned to work on the project full-time. They report directly to the project manager and not the home unit's head for the duration of the project.

On a day-to-day basis, the project manager is responsible for the entire lifecycle of the project from initiation, planning, execution, monitoring, to closure (Project Management Institute, 2021). The project manager reports to the project sponsor and steering committees on all project-related matters and coordinates the project team's activities. If an external consultant is hired, the project manager would have to work collaboratively with him or her for the completion of the project. The project manager is accountable for the overall project strategy, project implementation, project deliverables, and outcome. The project manager develops and administers the project plan with the aim of completing the project on time, on budget, and within scope. In the process, he or she conducts regular project meetings with the project team, external consultants, and vendors. The project team members are selected to represent different groups within the organization. They are expected to actively participate in project activities and contribute to the project deliverables. For larger and more complex projects, team leaders are assigned. These team leaders supervise separate workstreams, manage team member activities, and report to the project manager.

A competent project manager and performing project team are crucial factors affecting successful project conclusion. The project manager should have strong leadership, communication, negotiation, people, business, and technical skills among others. The incumbent is expected to manage the sequence of activities to transform inputs into outputs or outcomes that are of value to the receiver. The main responsibility of a project manager is to achieve the project objectives. Thus, establishing clear objectives is very important in project management. The project manager must also take into consideration all the other project goals such as quality, scope, time, and cost. Project teams are also an important consideration of project management practices. They are essential to the proper functioning of day-to-day project management activities. The main purpose of forming teams is to tap on the strengths of the individual and synergy of the group. Thus, the selection of the right project team members is a critical success factor. By creating a diverse team with a shared sense of purpose, more creative ideas can be generated to solve more complex problems. A performing team consists of individuals who complement each other and work together cooperatively to achieve project goals. The challenge is how to create such high-performing teams which contribute to project successes. A good practice is team empowerment. The organization and project sponsor would need to clearly express and define what team empowerment means. As far as possible, the boundaries for decision-making for the project should be clarified so that the project team is aware of the limits to their power. While the executive management and project sponsor are responsible for the overall strategic direction of the project and the project team is responsible for the tactical aspects, there are other areas such as quality objectives to be attained and access to additional organizational resources that should be made known. Only when the project team is clear about their area of authority would they be able to work confidently toward the project goals. On a related note, ongoing executive management participation and involvement are crucial to project success. While the project team should be given the freedom to run the project, the executive management and project sponsor must keep communication channels open and intervene whenever necessary. They must help the project team to resolve any issues or problems faced that are beyond the project team's area of responsibility or authority. The project team should not be left on their own to tackle these challenges.

There are several major activities and key tasks during the project lifecycle which must be performed well to ensure smooth transitions between the project phases. For example, at the beginning of the project lifecycle, the project manager must produce a project initiation document which contains the initial project plan and the underlying business case. During the planning phase, additional details are added to better define the project. This project plan should cover areas such as project scope, requirements, schedule, risks, and resources while the business case includes the justifications for embarking on the project and the associated benefits to be reaped. It is important to define the key milestones and risks. In the execution phase, the project manager must meet frequently with the project team, monitor the project progress, and provide updates to the steering committee. The project team members would be implementing the activities as highlighted in the detailed project plans. These detailed project plans contain discrete areas of work with specific objectives relating to the overall project plan. Project managers typically use a work breakdown structure to decompose all the necessary activities to produce the project deliverables.

During implementation, the project manager should always maintain clear communication with all the relevant parties. The project team members should also keep each other updated on the progress in their respective areas of work. Individuals and teams should encourage a free flow of ideas and actively solicit inputs for better decision-making. For project monitoring, it is important to check project progress against objectives. Project quality is a critical area that should be considered right from the start of the project. This is to ensure that subsequent quality assurance and control activities could be carried out more efficiently and effectively (Verzuh, 2021). The project manager should institute control mechanisms to make sure that project budgets and costs are managed appropriately. The initial estimates could be derived from past projects or historical data. The risk register is a tool that must be continually updated before an issue becomes a problem hindering project progress. Another good practice is maintaining the integrity of project reporting and documentation. Such documentations should include weekly and monthly reports for the project sponsor, steering committee, and other key stakeholders. In some instances, a project management office could provide these services to the project manager. Finally, when the project is near completion, the project manager would have to prepare an end project report for formal review to determine project performance (Wysocki, 2019). A project closure document would also be prepared for final sign-off.

Finally, a few thoughts on common project pitfalls and how to prevent them from happening. Many organizations have been using projects to achieve specific business goals. Project management is a means for the organization to plan for resources and execute activities as part of its strategy. However, managing projects is not an easy task because there are many challenges associated with it, for example, poorly defined project goals, project scope creep, and a lack of project communication. Sometimes, a project is initiated with poorly defined goals because it is hastily introduced due to sudden changes in external market environment or other organizational requirements. This phenomenon is common among digital transformation initiatives. The lack of a clear direction and goals lead to much confusion in the planning and execution of the project among the team members. This is because they would not be able to exercise proper judgment to prioritize conflicting project goals such as quality, scope, time, and cost. Furthermore, the organization would also face difficulties determining how the project fits into the overall strategy. The specific project may not be aligned to the organization's long-term direction. To overcome such issues, executive management must take the lead to ensure that the digital transformation project is aligned to the overall strategy and creates business value, also that the digital solution addresses both the technical and operational needs of the organization and can be fully integrated into the existing business processes.

It is often said that projects take on a life of their own. The statement is particularly true when referring to the scope of a project. Many projects grow beyond what was initially planned because of frequent uncontrolled requirement changes and miscommunication among stakeholders. Scope creep is a common problem in projects. Although an organization should be responsive and proactive in adjusting the project plan and activities to accommodate changing business needs and market conditions, the extent of the changes requires careful attention. This is because scope creeps will result in project delays and budget overruns. To ensure project success, the project manager must determine the factors that affect project scope and weigh the cost and benefit before deciding to expand the scope of the project. The project manager should seek alignment among the key stakeholders and establish a common understanding in the final project deliverables to avoid unnecessary time delays and wastages of resources.

Effective communication is an essential skill for human interactions. In almost all situations, a lack of communication or miscommunication would certainly lead to unfavorable project outcomes. Poor communication could occur either among the project team members or outside the project teams with other stakeholders. The issues arising are normally related to the timeliness and transparency of communication. In general, team members and key stakeholders expect to receive relevant project information early and promptly. Furthermore, they should be receiving the information directly from the authorized project team member and not through the grapevine. Of course, it is also important to be transparent in communicating the reasons behind decisions so that everyone understands the motivation for the organization's actions. Without effective communication, conflicts would surface resulting in project failures.

CASE ILLUSTRATION

The Government Technology Agency of Singapore (GovTech) is an organization driving the country's public sector digital transformation initiatives. The organization works closely with other government units to develop digital products and services that improve the way citizens live, work, and play (Government Technology Agency, 2021). It adopts agile methods to build and scale digital platforms for nation-wide deployment. For example, through its Government Digital Services division, GovTech has developed various apps such as TraceTogether and GoBusiness Licensing (Government Digital Services, n.d.). TraceTogether is a Bluetooth peer-to-peer connection app which allows a user's close contacts to be identified during the COVID-19 pandemic. GoBusiness Licensing is a one-stop portal for business owners to apply for all the required licenses without having to visit multiple agencies. Government Digital Services is currently developing a Moments of Life app, which provides a single digital platform where the major life events of citizens are bundled into personalized services for ease of access. These achievements would not have been possible without GovTech's strong digital product management and development capability.

SUMMARY

This chapter focuses on the management of digital products and how they drive business growth. The digital product management role and function is clarified and explained. Broadly, it involves boundary-spanning activities to facilitate the flow of external market and customer information to internal stakeholders. To better understand the work of a digital product manager, a hypothetical case is used to illustrate the day-to-day activities. Some core competencies that are required to improve digital product management success are discussed. In the digital age, organizations require a mix of product and project management talents to succeed. The question is not about either or but how both roles can work collaboratively to deliver digital products and projects successfully. The main project management phases such as initiation, planning, execution, monitoring, to closure are described together with some advice on good practices. Although many organizations have been using projects to drive business goals, there are still many challenges to be overcome. Some suggestions on how to better manage projects are provided.

REFERENCES

Blosch, M., Brand, S., & Osmond, N. (2019). *Enterprise architects combine design thinking, lean start-up and Agile to drive digital innovation.* Gartner, Inc.

Broadcom. (2020). *Digital product management: Go beyond traditional projects to product-focused planning.* https://docs.broadcom.com/doc/Clarity-PPM-Digital-Product-Management-WP

Cerri. (2019). *The shift from project-based management to (digital) product-based management.* https://www.cerri.com/wp-content/uploads/2020/02/digital-product-based-management.pdf

Davenport, T. (2021). *The future of work now: Product managers at Shopee.* Forbes. https://www.forbes.com/sites/tomdavenport/2021/04/20/the-future-of-work-now-product-managers-at-shopee/?sh=772ad38e7df0

Geissbauer, R., Schrauf, S., Morr, J., Wunderlin, J. T., Krause, J. H., & Odenkirchen, A. (2019). *Digital product development 2025: Agile, collaborative, AI driven, and customer centric.* PricewaterhouseCoopers. https://www.pwc.de/de/digitale-transformation/pwc-studie-digital-product-development-2025.pdf

Gnanasambandam, C., Harrysson, M., Srivastava, S., & Wu, Y. (2017). *Product managers for the digital world.* McKinsey & Company. https://www.mckinsey.com/industries/technology-media-and-telecommunications/our-insights/product-managers-for-the-digital-world#

Government Digital Services. (n.d.). *Helping citizens one idea at a time.* Government of Singapore. https://www.hive.tech.gov.sg/

Government Technology Agency. (2021, October 1). *Our role.* Government of Singapore. https://www.tech.gov.sg/who-we-are/our-role/

Jelen, T. (2019). *What does a digital product manager do?* Delcor. https://www.delcor.com/resources/blog/what-does-a-digital-product-manager-do

Kawamura, J., Schroeck, M., & Kwan, A. (2019). *Digital product management: A structured approach to product innovation and governance.* Deloitte. https://www2.deloitte.com/us/en/insights/focus/industry-4-0/product-innovation-and-governance.html

Layon, K. (2014). *Digital product management: Design websites and mobile apps that exceed expectations*. New Riders.

ProductPlan. (n.d.). *Career guide for product managers.* http://assets.productplan.com/content/career-guide-for-product-managers-by-productplan.pdf

Project Management Institute. (2021). *A guide to the project management body of knowledge* (7th ed.). Project Management Institute.

Verzuh, E. (2021). *The fast forward MBA in project management: The comprehensive, easy-to-read handbook for beginners and pros.* John Wiley & Sons, Inc.

Wysocki, R. (2019). *Effective project management: Traditional, agile, extreme, hybrid* (8th ed.). John Wiley & Sons, Inc.

6

Agile and DevSecOps

In today's era of volatility, there is no other way but to re-invent. The only sustainable advantage you can have over others is agility, that's it. Because nothing else is sustainable, everything else you create somebody else will replicate.

Jeff Bezos, Amazon

MOVING QUICKLY AND EASILY

Without a doubt, organizations are experiencing unprecedented rate of change. The effect is felt both outside and inside the organization. Externally, it impacts the way the organization interacts with customers. Internally, employees must completely alter the way they work. Thus, organizations need to be highly responsive to customer needs and feedback as well as agile in managing work. They should adopt a more flexible management style to implement digital transformation projects. The goal is to become nimbler in systems analysis and design beyond a linear sequential flow of activities to enable digital transformation. One approach is to embrace a rapid development technique in which actions happen alongside each other and that versions of an application are released in an iterative manner. While trying to stay ahead of external changes, organizations should design internal change management programs to influence how employees behave and operate. They need a strategic and structured approach to manage these organizational behavioral changes. These interventions should keep pace with the external changes so that the organization can continue to compete successfully.

DOI: 10.1201/9781003311393-7

The traditional waterfall approach to software development is not sufficiently adaptable to deliver business results fast. The waterfall method considers the steps of a project as separate and distinct phases. A typical waterfall model has the following phases: requirements, design, implementation, verification, and maintenance. Prior approval for one phase must be obtained before moving to the next phase. If a new necessity is found in the design phase, the process must go back to the initial requirements phase for the records to be altered and approved. The underlying assumption is that each phase can be completed with minimal changes to the phase before it. Despite the emphasis on a linear sequence of phases, in practice, there are always many iterations between these phases. Project changes are bound to happen and can derail the original plan and schedule. The specification of distinct phases with fixed checkpoints makes this approach unresponsive to evolving user requirements. It is highly rigid and less suitable for digital transformation projects which involve frequent changes.

The Agile way breaks down bigger projects into smaller blocks which are more manageable. Each small block goes through an iteration to produce a version of the product called minimum viable product (MVP), which is of value to the user. An MVP is a potentially shippable product that can add to the return on investment. The user gives some suggestions to improve the product, and these go into the next iteration. Under this methodology, designers, software developers, and business units work together collaboratively and simultaneously. To further support quick version releases, the organization would at times downplay formal project signoffs and overly detailed documentation. Small teams and members with formally defined roles are physically co-located near each other. The proximity among the members boosts collaboration and lowers the need to record every single detail when designing, developing, and testing the products (Ravichandran et al., 2016). For each fully functioning release, the business side or user will provide their inputs, and this information is used as the next iteration in the next release. Thus, each version is built iteratively and incrementally until the final draft is ready. The practices help to significantly cut down the number of delays in digital transformation projects.

AGILE PRINCIPLES AND IMPLEMENTATION

The Agile Manifesto highlights four values, namely, 'individuals and interactions over processes and tools', 'working software over comprehensive documentation', 'customer collaboration over contract negotiation', and 'responding to change over following a plan' to help organize software development activities (Agile Alliance, 2001). These statements suggest that some factors deserve more attention than others and do not mean that the least preferred considerations should be replaced. For example, processes and tools are still required in a software development project. However, they should not take precedence over individuals and interactions.

The manifesto also includes 12 principles that provide guidance to how software development projects should be implemented (Agile Alliance, 2001). The first four principles are 'our highest priority is to satisfy the customer through early and continuous delivery of valuable software', 'welcome changing requirements, even late in development (Agile processes harness change for the customer's competitive advantage)', 'deliver working software frequently, from a couple of weeks to a couple of months, with a preference to the shorter timescale', and 'business people and developers must work together daily throughout the project'. The next four principles are 'build projects around motivated individuals (give them the environment and support they need and trust them to get the job done)', 'the most efficient and effective method of conveying information to and within a development team is face-to-face conversation', 'working software is the primary measure of progress', and 'Agile processes promote sustainable development (the sponsors, developers, and users should be able to maintain a constant pace indefinitely)'. The last four principles are 'continuous attention to technical excellence and good design enhances agility', 'simplicity – the art of maximizing the amount of work not done – is essential', 'the best architectures, requirements, and designs emerge from self-organizing teams', and at 'regular intervals, the team reflects on how to become more effective, then tunes and adjusts its behavior accordingly'. These propositions serve as the foundation on which Agile practices are developed and implemented.

The actual implementation of Agile values and principles comes in various 'flavors' or types of methodology. Some of these techniques include Scrum, Kanban, and eXtreme Programing (XP) (Stellman et al., 2014). In rugby, a scrum involves players huddled together with their heads down to gain possession of the ball. In a similar way, it is like a development team working collaboratively to deliver an application. Briefly, a Scrum project is broken down into iterative cycles called sprints (Agh & Ramsin, 2021; Schwaber & Sutherland, 2020). At the initial kickoff meeting, the user defines the product features, and a project backlog is created. Before each sprint, the goals are determined, and a diverse team will proceed to execute the activities. During the sprint, the team does not communicate with the user and no new requirements are added. Every morning, each member of the team is asked three standard questions, 'What did you do yesterday?', 'What are you going to do today?', and 'Are there any impediments in your way?'. These questions ensure transparency and accountability in their daily work. Also, if there is anything that hinders the job, a fast resolution can be provided by the Scrum master. On the completion of a sprint, the work produced will be reviewed by the product owner from a business perspective. Suggestions for improvements would be incorporated into the next sprint.

Kanban is two Japanese words combined to mean visual board. Consequently, Kanban relies heavily on the visualization of the workflow to accomplish a project (Leopold & Kaltenecker, 2015). Project development is based on the roadmap as represented on whiteboards and sticky notes. This method limits the scope by prioritizing work in progress to match the team's capacity. There are no standard procedures or fixed iterations to follow. As soon as a task is complete, the team can take the next item from the pipeline. The team can do small pieces of work as they arise and make small releases which adapt to changing priorities. The main advantages are flexibility, transparency, clear objectives, and quicker turnaround time during development. The Kanban approach is more evolutionary than revolutionary in nature. XP focuses on customer satisfaction and requires maximum customer interaction. The emphasis is on the engineering aspect of software development to help developers write better codes. XP divides the entire software development life cycle into short cycles (Stellman et al., 2014). Changes in requirements can be incorporated at any phase of the life cycle. At the initial phase, user requirements are collected. Then, the requirements are prioritized and the number of smaller cycles determined. During the development phase, the developers work in pairs on a single program. This pair programing method requires one developer to write the codes and the other to check for computer errors or bugs. Extensive code review is a key feature of XP as a form of quality assurance to identify and rectify mistakes. The iteration begins and is adjusted when new requirements are added. The latest version of the program is user tested and accepted before the next iteration starts. In addition, the developers also use a process called code refactoring, where the existing computer code is redesigned and restructured while keeping its functionality.

BRING TOGETHER SOFTWARE DEVELOPMENT AND IT OPERATIONS

Most organizations face many challenges in managing software delivery. For example, the traditional software delivery methods may be too slow for today's speed of doing digital business. Also, there could be a lot of unnecessary reworks due to defects being only revealed at the later stages of production. Furthermore, the additional efforts channeled to create functionalities are not required for the MVP. Some of these complications may be partly due to information technology (IT) teams operating in silos and the many manual processes involved (Farooqui, 2018). The centralization and specialization of various IT functions exacerbate the problem because releases must be in a queue for each of the services provided. Consequently, organizations must relook at ways to minimize bottlenecks in the software delivery lifecycle to make it more efficient and effective.

DevOps is an approach that brings together software development (Dev) and IT operations (Ops) to optimize and manage end-to-end service delivery and operations (Ebert et al., 2016). It emphasizes incremental value delivery and process optimization including continuous improvement. DevOps applies Agile principles and utilizes technology tools to accelerate product or service delivery from ideation to production release to enhancements following customer feedback. It is quite common that the right feedback is not received sufficiently early for teams to respond with quality inputs. By breaking the digital project into smaller parts and releasing them as soon as they are complete, customer feedback can be sought early, and further improvements can be made. By actively eliminating waste in the activities, the process becomes more efficient, and costs are reduced.

An important idea is the shift left concept where certain tasks are done as soon as possible to identify and prevent defects early in the software delivery process to improve overall quality. For example, an application should be tested in an environment that represents a near-actual production environment for performance and quality assurance. This practice allows both the application as well as the application delivery process to be tested and validated ahead of time. Doing so benefits both the software development and IT operations teams. This allows the organization to react and make changes more rapidly. The software development side can re-adjust project priorities, the IT operations can improve the production environment, and the business side can revise the release timeline.

Through DevOps, business value is greatly enhanced when the speed of application releases to production increases with a shortened time to market. However, it is not a simple task to balance the somewhat opposing goals of software development and IT operations. The former strives toward fast delivery of applications, while the latter aims for systems stability and resilience. On the one hand, software development may view some due diligence procedures as hindrances that slow down coding activities. On the other hand, IT operations may believe that fast delivery must be properly managed in a stable production environment. While the friction that exists is not all that bad, it does present some challenges to an organization wanting to rapidly deploy digital products to stay ahead of competition. One solution is to create multi-disciplinary teams. With a multi-disciplinary team structure, software development and IT operations staff can work together closely and continuously deliver high-quality digital products by incorporating customer feedback at a faster pace. In general, software projects require the involvement of large numbers of people from business, operations, and IT. These employees must also work with external parties such as vendors and suppliers. All these parties are likely to be located across various sites. Since close collaboration among stakeholders is crucial to meet the tight deadlines, a multi-disciplinary team consisting of software development and IT operations staff can be formed and co-located. This arrangement helps to improve coordination and reduces inefficiencies while working on a digital project. It allows more complex and interdependent issues to be addressed from different viewpoints. Competing perspectives can be reconciled quickly to improve overall business outcomes. Beyond the change in organization structure, a culture of collaboration and shared responsibility, and an end-to-end ownership of services are also encouraged (Lwakatare et al., 2019). This means that both functions must work closely together in the creation of the deliverables and are responsible from the beginning until completion of the digital project. As part of the collaboration, the DevOps team must establish mutually agreeable targets and project timelines.

Automation is necessary to reduce the time taken to complete a task. It is the basis which enables a process to be reliable and repeatable. In addition, automation facilitates iterations and constant delivery of tasks. With automation, DevOps teams can deploy tests more frequently to detect errors early for rectifications (Ambily, 2020). This significantly lowers the risk of implementation failures at release time. Continuous testing means testing the product earlier and continuously across the software development life cycle. Instead of doing these activities later when the application is near completion, they are built-in early in the process. Besides automated testing, the DevOps team may implement service virtualization which makes continuous testing feasible. Through service virtualization, a simulated component which bears the characteristics of a real component is deployed to test the application. Automation also permits continuous integration and continuous delivery (Leite et al. 2020). In continuous integration, developers would regularly merge their code changes into a central repository where tests on the integrated work are run automatically. It involves the testing, verification, and validation of the code produced among the developers, and with other aspects of the application. The practice can be extended to cover complex systems made up of multiple systems or services where the integrated work could be tested as well. Similarly, routine integration helps to detect integration problems prior, thereby reducing the risk of rework subsequently. In continuous delivery, the code changes are automatically built, tested, and prepared for a release to production. It is a step-up of continuous integration where the continuous release and deployment of the application creates a delivery pipeline to production automatically.

Monitoring is another major DevOps activity. Unlike traditional approaches, DevOps advocates monitoring earlier in the life cycle through automated testing of functional and non-functional elements. Continuous monitoring provides vital information about the product at different stages of the software development life cycle. For example, the organization could check how the released applications are performing in production. Customer feedback such as usage patterns and pain points are collected. The quality metrics captured could be analyzed. This information allows the organization to adjust the actual digital project schedule and business plans accordingly. These metrics are not limited to the production stage only but are required at the other stages as well. Regular monitoring of performance prevents poor functioning of the application at production since any operational issue would have been flagged out upfront. Essentially, continuous monitoring functions as a repeated feedback loop which helps the organization to be agile and responsive to customer needs.

The ability to scale a business is a key differentiator for digital transformation. Scaling is important because it allows an organization to raise revenue exponentially without having a corresponding increase in costs.

If the teams have already adopted some form of Agile principles and practices and wish to scale at the enterprise level, they can consider frameworks such as Scaled Agile Framework (SAFe), Scrum of Scrums, Large Scale Scrum (LeSS), and Disciplined Agile (DA). These frameworks provide guidance in adopting Agile organization wide. They go beyond software and code development to include other areas such as enterprise architecture and digital governance. The coverage also includes executive management roles. In short, the principles and practices that have worked well at the team level are now extended and applied at the organization level. In the choice of frameworks, it is important to note that each has its own unique features, pros, and cons. Thus, the organization must understand its needs and apply the appropriate one to maximize the benefits. Some selection factors to consider include the stage of the Agile journey which the organization is in and the organization's readiness to collectively embrace Agile. Regardless of the framework picked, the organization will have to institutionalize autonomous teams and align Agile values including accountability and transparency across the organization.

ADDING THE IT SECURITY COMPONENT

Digital data transfer is commonplace among organizations. With the growth in the value of information, computer hackers are always on the lookout to exploit vulnerabilities in software systems. At the same time, organizational reliance on applications has also been increasing in a digital era. It is almost impossible to carry out any daily operations without using an IT system. Thus, IT security becomes crucial in protecting these vital IT assets. Nevertheless, IT security is often an afterthought in software development. It is usually considered in the later stages of the software development lifecycle. Furthermore, with the introduction of DevOps for rapid software development, the ability to deploy applications has increased in both speed and scale. Given these scenarios, IT security specialists must accelerate their efforts to keep pace with the fast rollout of software products.

DevSecOps is an approach aimed at unifying software development (Dev), IT security (Sec), and IT operations (Ops) (Ribeiro, 2022). It integrates the IT security element into DevOps practices. The collaboration involves software development, IT operations, and IT security teams.

Security protocols are incorporated into the software development lifecycle. Thus, the key benefits of DevOps which include agility and responsiveness are now being extended with the addition of the IT security component. The main characteristics of DevSecOps are to automate, monitor, and employ security throughout the software development lifecycle (Zeeshan, 2020).

In DevSecOps, all the IT security and testing activities are shifted to the left and performed upfront in the software development lifecycle. Just as it is less expensive to repair errors earlier in the software development lifecycle, it is also easier to apply IT security fixes as soon as possible. In this way, all the functional and IT security features are built and tested simultaneously. For example, in a typical workflow, once a software developer has created a set of codes, another developer will review it for IT security problems. Upon clearing the static code analysis, it will automatically be set up in a system with the relevant tests including IT security test being conducted. Passing these tests results in these codes moving into a production environment for monitoring. If IT security threats are uncovered, they will be rectified with a new set of codes being developed. The process is then repeated. Some of the other good DevSecOps practices include integrating automated security testing into the pipeline, continuous monitoring, and remediating application security vulnerabilities (Dang & Kohgadai, 2021). To integrate automated IT security testing into the pipeline is to incorporate computerized security assessment into the various phases such as build and deployment. Continuous monitoring is to track performance to uncover security problems for the prevention of breaches. In remediating application security vulnerabilities, clear plans should be developed that can be executed immediately to remove any weaknesses.

TRANSFORMING ORGANIZATIONAL CULTURE

Organizations are beginning to realize that existing assumptions and past practices to manage employees are inadequate in a rapidly changing digital world. The traditional mechanistic model of the organization is not able to meet the challenges of a fast-moving market. Driving efficiency through optimized processes and automation alone will not be sufficient to solve complex problems. Relying on linear thinking and control creates more problems than solutions. The command-and-control style of work is not effective to ensure predictability of business results. Organizations require a new operating model in response to a more complex and uncertain environment. In the face of uncertainties, strong employee connections and interactions can help the organizations better prepare for the future. Enhancing employee interactions promotes creativity and innovation. Through improved employee networks and working relationships, an organization will be better positioned to overcome business problems, generate creative ideas, and launch new products and services. One solution is to adopt a more organic and non-linear approach to working by promoting stronger interactions and collaborations among employees. For example, Agile practices could be featured more prominently as part of the organizational culture. However, in opting to implement Agile methodologies and the corresponding automated tools, it is critical to consider the people side of change. How the employees behave and respond to business changes will have a huge impact on overall success. These behaviors, in turn, are driven to a large extent by the organization's culture and vice versa.

An organization's culture defines how people are expected to behave in certain ways in a corporate setting (Groysberg et al., 2018). It arises from the set of core values and beliefs held by a group of people working together (Baumgartner, 2020). These implicit assumptions shape the way the members behave and their interactions with each other. These tacit views manifest into observable norms and practices that affect organizational structures, processes, and systems. To be successful in the implementation of Agile projects, executive management needs to build an organizational culture to support these activities (Walker & Soule, 2017). They must communicate the desired values and reinforce them through organizational policies and procedures. These practices must be promoted at every level of the hierarchy. A mindset change toward the Agile way is required at all levels of the organization from the executive management to the middle management and to the rank and file (Cram, 2019).

The executive management team is responsible for providing strong leadership in digital transformation. The leaders must be able to inspire and motivate the rest of the organization to achieve the shared vision and organizational goals. Then, translate and cascade these high-level goals into group- and individual-level objectives. To do so, they must clearly communicate the requirements to every level of the organization so that employees know specifically what the targets are to be achieved. At the same time, executive management must play an active role in driving Agile values and principles across the entire organization. They must coach major Agile teams and mentor key individuals (Denning, 2020). Furthermore, executive management must understand that these values and principles very often operate contrary to established management practices (Shore & Warden, 2021). These management practices include top-down authority and routine activities such as formal management reporting, periodic project meetings, and detailed progress documentation.

To build an Agile culture, the executive management must focus on values and practices which promote collaboration and knowledge sharing among employees. There should be an inclusive environment where different views are respected and considered for the good of the organization. Open communication where employees can freely express their ideas and not be afraid of speaking up for fear of upsetting anyone must be encouraged. In this context, trust plays a critical role in fostering a collaborative culture. Trust is the foundation which human activities are built on. Employees must feel safe working with one another at the workplace. In addition, executive management should promote a growth mindset among employees to share information. Groups must refrain from keeping project information to themselves. Instead, such information should be made available to all the relevant parties so that there is visibility about the project status. This would ensure that every team member is on the same page and is working toward the same organizational goals. A common cause of employee resistance to organizational change is the fear of failure. When a project or assigned task fails, the individual may feel a 'loss of face' and think that his or her career advancement will be affected. Thus, executive management needs to be more tolerant toward project failures since they are an integral part of innovation. In addition, executive management could regularly reinforce a message of innovation and experimentation. One way to encourage innovation through experimentation is giving credit and recognizing those who introduce new ideas as well as those who make mistakes in the process of experimenting.

For the middle management and rank and file, Agile practices require a high degree of collaboration across different roles and departments. For this to happen, certain job roles may have to be redefined to facilitate teamwork and collaborative behaviors. A good starting point is the formation of cross-functional groups. Take the case of a traditional IT department, where teams are organized into 'technical silos' such as software development, IT security, and IT operations. A cross-functional group could be formed among these technical teams together with some representatives from the business units to work toward a common project goal. Training and competency development is another important consideration. To implement DevSecOps practices, each specific IT team must be equipped with the necessary competencies. The organization should not assume that the different IT teams have common technical knowledge that spans across areas such as software development, IT security, and IT operations. The developers and IT engineers who do not specialize in IT security may have limited knowledge of identity and access management. Similarly, an IT security architect may not be familiar with software development concepts such as containerization and hashing. Thus, the former group would have to attend fundamental security awareness training such as denial of service attacks and tampering techniques to be able to recognize these actions and understand the implications. For the IT security team, they need to be aware of different software development lifecycle phases such as requirement collection, design, coding, and deployment. More importantly, to be able to appreciate the implications when specific software modifications are made.

A strong organizational culture is a positive factor and necessary condition to drive performance. While organizational culture is manifested through employee behaviors, true change does not happen when new behaviors are imposed. Only when the organizational values and the meanings are shared by most of the employees will the change be permanent. Thus, the organization must avoid quick fixes and imposing norms without inculcating these values among the employees. To do this well, a lot of time and effort is needed. The organization needs to have persistence to promote culture change over the long run.

CASE ILLUSTRATION

In 2018, the Development Bank of Singapore (DBS) was recognized by Euromoney as the World's Best Digital Bank for the second time (Development Bank of Singapore, 2018). The first time which the bank received the accolade was two years earlier. These awards recognize the bank's concerted efforts and numerous achievements in digital innovation. One area which enabled DBS to better serve its customers is by adopting DevOps practices (Huxley Associates, n.d.). The various development, operations, testing, and quality assurance teams can collaborate more effectively, thereby, shortening systems development life cycle and ensuring a continual stream of quality applications for the customers. These practices lay a strong foundation for the bank to be able to move quickly and easily in the digital landscape. Consequently, the bank can compete more effectively and build better digital platforms to better serve customer needs around the region.

SUMMARY

This chapter highlights the Agile approach and practices for software development. It describes some of the shortcomings of the traditional waterfall method and how Agile can address these weaknesses more effectively. Some of the advantages in adopting Agile practices include faster digital product delivery which better meets customer needs, lowering of project risk because flaws can be detected early, and improving the overall quality since even small improvements in the digital product are tested often. DevOps brings together software development and IT operations activities with automation. When the security component is included, the set of practices is known as DevSecOps. To build strong Agile teams, it is imperative to focus on an organizational culture which promotes Agile values, mindset, and behaviors. A strong organizational culture would influence the way people work and respond to changes. This, in turn, would allow the organization to become more responsive and competitive in the digital age.

REFERENCES

Agh, H., & Ramsin, R. (2021). Scrum metaprocess: A process line approach for customizing Scrum. *Software Quality Journal, 29*(2), 337–379. https://doi.org/10.1007/s11219-021-09551-4

Agile Alliance. (2001). *The Agile manifesto.* Agile Alliance. https://www.agilealliance.org/agile101/the-agile-manifesto/

Ambily, K. K. (2020). *Azure DevOps for web developers: Streamlined application development using Azure DevOps features* (1st ed.). Apress. https://doi.org/10.1007/978-1-4842-6412-6

Baumgartner, N. (2020). *Build a culture that aligns with people's values.* Harvard Business Review. https://hbr.org/2020/04/build-a-culture-that-aligns-with-peoples-values

Cram, W. A. (2019). Agile development in practice: Lessons from the trenches. *Information Systems Management, 36*(1), 2–14. https://doi.org/10.1080/10580530.2018.1553645

Dang, W. L., & Kohgadai, A. (2021). *DevSecOps in Kubernetes*. O'Reilly Media, Inc.

Denning, S. (2020). How the C-suite is embracing Agile. *Strategy & Leadership, 48*(5), 19–24. https://doi.org/10.1108/SL-06-2020-0084

Development Bank of Singapore. (2018). *DBS: The 50 years*. Development Bank of Singapore. https://www.dbs.com/livemore/uploads/DBS-The-50-years.pdf?pid=sg-group-pweb-about-slideupbanner-dbs-the-50-years

Ebert, C., Gallardo, G., Hernantes, J., & Serrano, N. (2016). DevOps. *IEEE Software, 33*(3), 94–100. https://doi.org/10.1109/MS.2016.68

Farooqui, S. M. (2018). *Enterprise DevOps framework transforming IT operations* (1st ed.). Apress. https://doi.org/10.1007/978-1-4842-3612-3

Groysberg, B., Lee, J., Price, J., & Cheng, Y.-J. (2018). *The leader's guide to corporate culture*. Harvard Business Review. https://hbr.org/2018/01/the-leaders-guide-to-corporate-culture

Huxley Associates. (n.d.). *DevOps within Singapore's banking and finance industry*. Huxley. https://www.huxley.com/en-sg/blog/2017/08/devops-within-singapores-banking-and-finance-industry/

Leite, L., Rocha, C., Kon, F., Milojicic, D., & Meirelles, P. (2020). A survey of DevOps concepts and challenges. *ACM Computing Surveys, 52*(6), 1–35. https://doi.org/10.1145/3359981

Leopold, K., & Kaltenecker, S. (2015). *Kanban change leadership: Creating a culture of continuous improvement*. John Wiley & Sons, Inc.

Lwakatare, L. E., Kilamo, T., Karvonen, T., Sauvola, T., Heikkilä, V., Itkonen, J., Kuvaja, P., Mikkonen, T., Oivo, M., & Lassenius, C. (2019). DevOps in practice: A multiple case study of five companies. *Information and Software Technology, 114*, 217–230. https://doi.org/10.1016/j.infsof.2019.06.010

Ravichandran, A., Taylor, K., & Waterhouse, P. (2016). *DevOps for digital leaders: Reignite business with a modern DevOps-enabled software factory*. Apress. https://doi.org/10.1007/978-1-4842-1842-6_3

Ribeiro, M. (2022). *Learning DevSecOps*. O'Reilly Media, Inc.

Schwaber, K., & Sutherland, J. (2020). *The scrum guide*. ScrumGuides.org. https://scrumguides.org/docs/scrumguide/v2020/2020-Scrum-Guide-US.pdf#zoom=100

Shore, J., & Warden, S. (2021). *The art of Agile development* (2nd ed.) O'Reilly Media, Inc.

Stellman, A., Greene, J., & Volckhausen, E. (2014). *Learning agile understanding Scrum, XP, Lean, and Kanban* (1st ed.). O'Reilly.

Walker, B., & Soule, S. (2017). *Changing company culture requires a movement, not a mandate*. Harvard Business Review. https://hbr.org/2017/06/changing-company-culture-requires-a-movement-not-a-mandate

Zeeshan, A. A. (2020). *DevSecOps for .NET core: Securing modern software Applications*. Apress.

7

Digital Enterprise Architecture

The next 5 years will be more disruptive than the last 15. This is not business as usual. A lot of technology that came in three years ago doesn't work anymore.

Saul Berman, IBM

BUSINESS AND IT ALIGNMENT

Organizations leverage information technology (IT) to enable a variety of business objectives, for example, to improve process efficiency, meet changing customer demands, or create new business opportunities. To fully realize the benefits, the organization must take a holistic view of business and IT and ensure that both domains are tightly aligned. Many digital transformation initiatives fail because of a misalignment of business objectives and IT priorities. Therefore, achieving a clear alignment between business objectives and IT priorities is important for organizations embarking on a digital transformation journey. The successful delivery of digital business outcomes requires strong collaboration between the business and technical teams in the organization (Hohpe, 2020).

An enterprise architecture (EA) blueprint is often used as a tool to bridge the gap between business strategy and technology implementation (Alaeddini et al., 2017). The EA provides a link to align business objectives and IT priorities. It functions as an essential technology component that augments the other digital transformation capabilities such as strategy, people, and process. Without a doubt, business drivers will always guide and direct the EA. For example, if the business driver is to promote a

DOI: 10.1201/9781003311393-8

remote workforce, then the EA design must be able to support consistent and comprehensive access of data by the employees from any location.

The EA development process facilitates the effective and efficient collaboration between the business and IT functions. It strengthens the organizational capability for service delivery. In the process of developing the digital EA, the organization would also review its strategic and IT plans against existing IT capabilities. At the same time, the organization can re-evaluate its digital transformation strategy and core processes. The gaps identified would be used to update the IT plan so that new IT capabilities can be built subsequently. The purpose is to ensure that the IT capabilities deployed can deliver the expected business value.

Organizations must strive to better integrate business and IT to deliver business value. Technology gaps can be easily bridged if business and IT have a clear understanding of the vision for digital transformation and clearly define the key organizational elements to achieve it. The approach is to establish a robust digital EA framework to align business processes and digital capabilities. It must be a strategic and enterprise-wide view of the entire ecosystem covering both business and IT domains. Furthermore, the organization must ensure that the teams have the required business acumen and technical competencies to collaborate to deal with the problems arising. While experienced enterprise architects and IT engineers can be recruited to manage and maintain the EA, it is essential that the non-technical managers understand some EA fundamentals, especially in relation to digital transformation. It will be useful to develop an appreciation of basic EA principles and the different types of architecture in an organization.

AN ENTERPRISE-WIDE VIEW

Broadly, EA is a term that can be applied to both the process and the outcome of specifying the overall structure, logical components, and interrelationships between the business and IT aspects (Open Group, 2018; Perez-Castillo et al., 2019). It defines how all pieces of an organization's computing system work together in support of the business strategy. EA is the overall design of the system of hardware, software, and data of an organization and is a blueprint of the organization's business and information systems. Various entities such as The Open Group and Gartner have provided definitions to better articulate the EA concept (Gampfer et al., 2018; Iyamu, 2018; Open Group, 2018). In some cases, the EA is described as a management practice for aligning resources to improve business performance. It consolidates the rationale for the core business processes and IT capabilities arising from the need to standardize and integrate them into the operating model. An EA helps to illustrate how the various digital systems and assets are logically structured and connected. Arising from this business and IT relationship, some digital EA principles such as maximizing interoperability and reusability of IT components can be formulated to guide decision-making. Other similar descriptions include EA as a blueprint that provides a holistic view of the business functions, data standards, and IT systems and services within the organization (Kotusev, 2019). Essentially, it is a conceptual blueprint of how the company organizes its IT assets. The EA provides the organization with a foundation for performing strategic planning and IT investment management. It is a plan for transitioning from the current state to the desired future state and provides direction for systems selection and design activities in support of business needs.

The benefits of digital EA adoption are many folds and become more apparent as the complexity and diversity of the business grow (Niemi & Pekkola, 2016; Shanks et al., 2018). At the fundamental level, a digital EA blueprint captures the key facts about the organization's processes and presents the information in an understandable way to facilitate better planning. The consistency, accuracy, and timeliness of the information shared across the organization help to improve decision-making. Executive management would gain a clearer view of the complexity of large systems, thereby, enhancing their understanding of business requirements and technology implementation. At a higher level, an EA defines the digital technology standards for everyone in the organization. This reduces duplication and diversity of requirements and facilitates interoperability of IT systems. It also creates more opportunities for building greater quality and flexibility into applications without increasing the cost. An EA helps to ensure that common IT components are used and shared across the organization. This leads to economies of scale since different ways for sharing services across the organization leveraging data, applications, and infrastructure are considered. The digital EA information can be used to analyze alternatives, risks, and trade-offs as part of the IT investment management process. Therefore, the EA is a very important part of digital transformation and organizations must apply these good practices using established frameworks.

ENTERPRISE ARCHITECTURE DOMAINS

A framework is used to provide the necessary structure to logically segment the organization's overall EA into domains or views. Some of the popular EA frameworks include The Open Group Architectural Framework (TOGAF), Zachman Framework for Enterprise Architecture, and Open Agile Architecture (Gampfer et al., 2018; Iyamu, 2018; Open Group, 2018). The implementation roadmap would differ depending on the type of EA framework selected by organization. In a simplified EA model, there are generally four domains that layer the overall architecture, namely, business architecture, data architecture, applications architecture, and technology architecture (Open Group, 2018).

The business architecture basically provides a representation of the organization's business strategy and key business processes. It gives a business perspective of the activities, standards, and rules by which the organization operates on a day-to-day basis. The information could include the organization's operating model, customer value proposition, and business capabilities. It also includes the core processes that are supported by the IT services and assets. These core processes could be depicted as part of a value chain diagram. The various organizational roles and relationships are incorporated to demonstrate the types of value delivered to the customers.

The data architecture covers areas such as data collection, data storage, and data utilization. It gives an information perspective of the definitions and classifications of data such as document files and images which the organization uses. The data architecture includes the organization's logical and physical data assets, also the data management resources. It comprises the entity's key information requirements and how these are derived, the common database shared by different applications, and business rules that governed the processes.

The applications architecture covers the software used to process data, including the interactions of procedures and standards. It defines the types of application systems necessary to process data and support the business. Primarily, the application architecture offers a view of the applications that have multiple technologies for enablement, intensity of usage of different applications, enterprise-wide versus unit-specific applications, and applications which require integration capabilities within and outside organizational boundaries. There are many types of applications that can be found in an organization, for example, a customer relationship management (CRM) system where an intelligent agent can automatically gather personalized information based on usage analysis. Also, an enterprise resource planning (ERP) system where the planning, manufacturing, sales and marketing functions, and processes are consolidated into one management system. Lastly, a supply chain management (SCM) system where the handling of the flow of goods, services and information across suppliers, manufacturers, wholesalers, and distributors all the way to the consumers can be optimized.

The technology architecture covers the various technologies such as hardware, operating systems, and networking solutions utilized by the organization. The technology architecture presents a view about the infrastructure and interaction of the platform services, and the logical and physical technology components. This is the domain which emphasizes the technologies or technical services used by the various applications. The infrastructure is the physical hardware and software used. The physical hardware is used to connect computers and users. This involves transmission media such as ethernet cables and routers and repeaters that control the transmission paths. The software is used to manage signals transmission. They include the operating systems used. The communication functions in the network need to be managed and coordinated. Other infrastructure details include those technologies supported by multiple vendors, used by different business processes, and the stage of development, namely emerging, current, or sunset, which the technology is deployed.

To illustrate the information pertaining to an EA, a case on how a hypothetical general insurance company segments its overall EA into the four domains is described next. For the business architecture domain, the information includes the company's organization structure consisting of a front office, back office, and shared service center; a value stream map covering the development of insurance products, marketing and sales of these products, management of policies and claims, and servicing of customers; a capability map containing business management, product management, asset management, money management, and policy claims management; business functions include marketing, actuarial and customer service; detailed business processes to manage policies and claims covering calculate insurance premium, issue new policy, and handle claims, just to name a few. For the application architecture domain, it contains a simple flow diagram of the linked applications serving a particular department. These applications include a web portal operated by the front office, a call center application, and a CRM system. In the data architecture domain, the view shows where the customer data resides in the customer records and files, similarly where the claim and policy data can be found in the respective claim and policy files. Finally, under the technology architecture domain, there are components such as front office web hosting server, general service server linked to the local area network (LAN), and the wide area network (WAN).

HOW INFORMATION TECHNOLOGY WORKS

Besides having a basic understanding of the four architecture domains, it is also useful to know how IT works in an organization, essentially, what is really happening inside the IT department and behind the doors of the chief information officer's office. The rest of the chapter will provide an overview of various key information system components, including basic hardware and software, network, data, IT security, and cloud computing. Hardware includes all the physical equipment used for computing. The common types of hardware are personal computers (PC), laptops, printers, data storage devices, servers, and backup appliances. In addition, some organizations also have mainframe computers as part of the hardware. Corporations build these mainframes mainly for large-scale data processing. These computers are associated with centralized rather than distributed computing because they are designed for one-way computing processes and are not interactive in nature. The role of the software is to instruct the hardware what to do. Software can be grouped into system software and application software. Microsoft Windows and Linux Operating System are two common examples of system software. Essentially, they provide instructions to a computer on how to run its most basic functions and interpret user commands. Application software is designed for specific tasks, such as creating presentation slides or designing a web page.

A special type of software is the middleware. A middleware connects and allows several processes running on multiple systems to interact across a network. In essence, it bridges the gap between applications and databases so that users can receive unified services across the entire organization. Like a middleware, enterprise application integration (EAI) also connects applications through a central message routing hub. However, it acts more like a central command center for integration within an enterprise system. This is because EAI tools are equipped to parse and translate data, and automatically route information according to business processes. Parsing is the conversion of data from one type to another.

Middleware is crucial in providing for communication across heterogeneous platforms because it has a more functional set of application programming interfaces (API). An API is a software intermediary that allows two applications to speak to each other. It is a set of conditions that control the communication and interactions between applications. Once the code for the software has been written, the API can execute the defined actions. It is not necessary to re-write the software each time these actions are performed. This not only reduces the amount of programming work required but also permits fast access to data. APIs are used to interact with IT elements such as operating systems and microservices. Many organizations extend their data and APIs to external parties to develop digital solutions. This requires the organization to make public the access to its proprietary applications and involves a relook at the organization's API strategy. A recent software trend is the move from a monolithic to microservices architecture. A monolithic application is generally built as a single unit with three parts, namely, client interface, server application, and database. For any alterations to happen in the system, an updated version of the entire server-side application must be developed and deployed. On the other hand, a microservices architecture is more modular and 'liquid' because it makes use of microservices, API, and cloud computing.

NETWORKS

Hardware needs to be connected to form a communication network. These connections can be through ethernet cables, fiber optic cables, or wireless fidelity (Wi-Fi). An ethernet cable contains a solid copper core for data transmission, while a fiber optic cable contains strands of glass fibers thinner than hair and transports data in the form of light waves. A physical network construction includes parts such as hubs, bridges, switches, and routers. Depending on the spatial distance, it can be a LAN or a WAN. The network may carry voice, data, or both forms of signals. Also, it may either be a private or public network, depending on the level of access restriction. In some cases, the connection is called a virtual private network (VPN), where software is used to create a 'passageway' for the organization's private data traffic using the public network system. The network that is formed between various data storage machines is a called storage area network (SAN). Such networks can cope with heavy bandwidth demands of storage data and segregate storage traffic built specifically for storage needs. The bandwidth refers to the amount of data a network can transport in a certain period which is the capacity for rate of transfer. It is usually expressed in bits per second.

An application program is usually organized into three tiers, which are distributed to a different place in a network. The three tiers are workstation interface, business logic, and database. The workstation interface tier contains the programming that provides the graphical user interface and application-specific entry forms. The business logic tier is located on the LAN server and acts as the server for client requests from workstations. It determines what data is needed and where it is located. The database tier is where the information is stored and controls its management and access. The signal transmissions across a network are governed by protocols. A protocol is the set of communication rules used by end points to communicate in a connection.

On the internet, there are the TCP/IP protocols. The transmission control protocol (TCP) assembles files into smaller information packets that are transmitted over the internet and received by another TCP layer that reassembles them. The internet protocol (IP) handles the address part of each packet so that it gets to the right destination. The hypertext transfer protocol (HTTP) and file transfer protocol (FTP) have defined sets of rules which correspond with programs for communication on the internet. Voice over internet protocol (VoIP) is a technology that provides voice transmission services over the internet. Using this means helps users to avoid toll call charges from the long-distance carrier. To send through voice, the information must be separated into packets just like in data transmission. These packets are required to be sent and put back together in an efficient manner. Asynchronous transfer mode (ATM) is a network technology that arranges digital data into units and transmits them over a physical medium. ATM uses packet-switching and multiplexing technologies to transform the data, sound, and video into a single entity called a cell. ATM is a key component of the broadband Integrated Services Digital Network (ISDN). ISDN is a set of standards for transmitting data over telephone copper wire adopted by the Telecommunication Standardization Sector of the International Telecommunications Union (ITU-T).

Communication connections can also be through wireless fidelity (Wi-Fi). 'Wireless' means transmitting signals over invisible radio waves instead of through physical wires. On the wireless front, the wireless application protocol (WAP) is the set of instructions used to transfer data to wireless devices. Bluetooth is a short-range wireless specification that allows for radio connections between devices. 5G is the fifth-generation mobile network and the new global wireless standard after 1G, 2G, 3G, and 4G networks. 1G is the first generation of wireless that introduced analog systems transmitting over radio frequencies It is used mainly for voice and gave rise to the first cell phones. 2G is the second generation of wireless introduced digital encoding and text messaging. 3G is the third generation with greater speeds for multimedia data and voice transmissions. The current 4G is more than ten times faster than its predecessor. A 5G capability will help to overcome many latency issues faced by organizations today and totally transform the way things are done. For a start, 5G offers very high-speed connections and delivers data with superior quality. 5G will significantly enhance the capabilities provided by other digital technologies such as cloud computing, Internet of Things (IoT), and artificial intelligence.

DATA

Traditionally, data that are stored in the applications and systems are periodically pulled into a data warehouse for analysis to support decision-making. A data warehouse captures and stores data from varied sources which can be combined for analysis. A typical data warehouse consists of several layers as follow: an external database layer which processes data to support critical operational needs; an information access layer which an end user deals with directly; a data access layer for communication between the information access and external database layer; a data directory later which contains the metadata; a process management layer involved in scheduling tasks; an application messaging layer for transporting information around the network; a physical layer where the actual data used primarily for informational uses occurs; finally, a data staging layer where all the other necessary processes reside.

In a conventional data warehouse process, data are obtained from the online transaction processing (OLTP) applications for use by the analytical applications. OLTP is a class of programs that manages data entry and retrieval transactions. Data analysis involves three main activities, namely, extraction, transformation, and loading. In extraction, data is read from a specified source database and extracted into a desired subset of data. In transformation, the acquired data is converted to a desired state using rules with the other data. In loading, the resulting data is written to a target database. Online analytical processing (OLAP) enables users to extract and examine data from different points of view. For example, an analyst can opt to present a worksheet displaying the revenue figures of all the company's products sold in country A in the first quarter of the year and compare these figures to the second quarter and evaluate the performance in this country during the same periods the previous year. The reason why OLAP data can do this is that it is stored in a multidimensional database unlike those stored in relational database which is two-dimensional. A multidimensional database takes into consideration each data attribute such as geography, product, revenue, and time.

The process of converting raw data into insightful information is called data mining. The practice entails sorting through data to identify patterns and establish relationships. These parameters may include association by studying for patterns where one event is connected to another; classification by searching for new patterns; and clustering by finding groups of facts not previously known. Various methods may be used such as decision trees and artificial neural networks.

IT SECURITY

In a digitally connected world, IT security or cybersecurity is a critical component of the digital EA. In any open system, there exists risk of cyberattacks and data breaches (Kim & Solomon, 2018). There are many occurrences of cyberattacks to obtain sensitive corporate and personal data and disrupt business activities. These malicious actions can come from opportunistic individuals or professional hackers. Thus, an organization would always impose security controls to prevent unauthorized access to sensitive information.

Organizations can employ a series of methods and practices such as using security software to monitor IT resource utilization and controlling access to data to counter cyber threats. A commonly used technology to block unauthorized access to organization's systems is the firewall. A firewall is a set of related programs or hardware which is located at a network gateway server that protects the resources of a private network from users from other networks. A firewall can be erected to filter network traffic. Furthermore, by monitoring an employee's virtual desktop utilization behavior patterns, alerts can be raised when a baseline is breached. In this way, it can stop any intrusion accessing the internal systems and databases once any unusual traffic is detected. A public key infrastructure (PKI) is a technology for securely exchanging information between users and devices. This method involves publishing 'public keys' with cryptography and tracking 'expired keys'. Briefly, a certification authority will issue a digital document called a digital certificate. It contains details such as the holder's name, serial number, public key, and the document's expiration date. Such digital certificates are used in PKI to send and receive secure, encrypted messages.

Perhaps the biggest risk to IT security lies in human interactions. Vulnerabilities in IT security often manifest through employee activities inside the organization which hackers exploit to their advantage. Through social engineering, hackers can trick users to give away sensitive information or commit security mistakes. Some examples are phishing emails to steal login credentials and baiting which uses false promises to fool the email recipient. Employees play a major role in making the organization safe and secure from cyberattacks. Thus, employees need to be careful when utilizing the organization's IT resources and introducing external IT elements such as using their own personal computing devices in the office. Doing so will increase the chance of cyberattacks by external hackers. To cope with cyber threats, organizations need an enterprise-wide IT security plan to integrate business and technical controls, also, to adopt a high-level view of internet and physical security mechanisms that meet regulatory requirements and can overcome threat scenarios. These security considerations should be incorporated into the digital EA and business processes.

CLOUD COMPUTING

Cloud computing uses a network of remote servers hosted on the internet to provide computing power and data storage. With this technology, organizations can eliminate the need to purchase and maintain costly servers on-sites. The practice of cloud computing has significantly influenced many organizations' views of EA. There is a growing trend toward cloud computing, and many organizations are trying to do it right. To the group of technology natives, adopting cloud solutions is intuitive and a natural choice. However, there are still a handful of C-suite executives who require more convincing to move to cloud (Ghosh & Narain, 2021). IT security remains a main concern as there is a general lack of understanding of the security features of cloud computing. There is a fear of security breaches in the cloud in the event of a cyberattack. In general, for cloud computing, security is built around the application instead of the infrastructure whereas for on-premise hosting, security is developed around the infrastructure.

There are many benefits in putting the organization's IT assets on the cloud. The cloud can be harnessed to drive business innovations. It can also improve the deplorability, scalability, and resilience of IT systems. To adopt cloud computing, the organization needs to consider how it can complement the existing EA, in addition, address issues such as the type of cloud services and the cloud architecture to use and the security standards to accept. There are various types of cloud configuration such as private clouds, public clouds, and hybrid clouds. A private cloud is used solely by an organization, while a public cloud is shared with others. A hybrid cloud uses both a private and a public cloud. There is also a multicloud, where a combination of cloud services is provided by different cloud vendors to the organization.

In general, cloud vendors can provide three models of cloud services such as Software as a Service (SaaS), Platform as a Service (PaaS), and Infrastructure as a Service (IaaS). SaaS is managed by the third-party vendor and the customer simply uses the application through the internet without having to install anything. PaaS offers slightly more cloud components to the customer. By offering developer tools, the customer can create bespoke applications. For IaaS, even more cloud components such as middleware and operating systems are made available to the customer. Depending on scale of the business and organizational needs, different cloud configurations and services will bring about various advantages and disadvantages. Thus, the organization needs to consider carefully how it can utilize cloud services to optimize performance.

CASE ILLUSTRATION

AIA Group Limited is a life insurance and financial services provider in the Asia Pacific region (AIA Singapore, n.d.). AIA Singapore, a subsidiary of the group, recently launched an interactive point of sale system to help insurance representatives process policy applications faster (Microsoft Singapore, 2020). The system uses cloud computing as part of the digital EA to ensure scalability of the platform and optimization of resources. The new design is built based on open-source components, PaaS, and migration of legacy databases to the cloud. By adopting a hybrid configuration, the company can take advantage of the flexibility offered by these optimized IT resources and move more rapidly to meet customer needs.

SUMMARY

This chapter describes the importance of a digital EA to an organization. A digital EA helps to align business objectives and IT priorities, which ismproves decision-making. It provides an enterprise-wide view of the organization across the business and IT domains. This will enable the organization to optimize the use of IT resources and eliminate inefficiencies. There are four domains that layer the overall EA. The business architecture provides a representation of the organization's business strategy and key business processes. The data architecture covers areas such as data collection, data storage, and data utilization. The applications architecture defines the types of application systems necessary to process data and support the business. Lastly, the technology architecture presents a view about the infrastructure and interaction of the platform services, and the logical and physical technology components. The chapter also includes an overview of key information system components such as hardware and software, network, data, IT security, and cloud computing.

REFERENCES

AIA Singapore. (n.d.). *About AIA Singapore*. AIA Group Limited and its subsidiaries. https://www.aia.com.sg/en/about-aia.html

Alaeddini, M., Asgari, H., Gharibi, A., & Rad, M. R. (2017). Leveraging business-IT alignment through enterprise architecture: An empirical study to estimate the extents. *Information Technology and Management, 18*(1), 55–82. https://doi.org/10.1007/s10799-016-0256-6

Gampfer, F., Jürgens, A., Müller, M., & Buchkremer, R. (2018). Past, current and future trends in enterprise architecture: A view beyond the horizon. *Computers in Industry*, *100*, 70–84. https://doi.org/10.1016/j.compind.2018.03.006

Ghosh, B., & Narain, K. (2021). *What CEOs need to know about the cloud in 2021*. Harvard Business Review. https://hbr.org/2021/03/what-ceos-need-to-know-about-the-cloud-in-2021

Hohpe, G. (2020). *The software architect elevator: Redefining the architect's role in the digital enterprise*. O'Reilly Media, Inc.

Iyamu, T. (2018). Implementation of the enterprise architecture through the Zachman Framework. *Journal of Systems and Information Technology*, *20*(1), 2–18. https://doi.org/10.1108/JSIT-06-2017-0047

Kim, D., & Solomon, M. (2018). *Fundamentals of information systems security* (3rd ed.). Jones & Bartlett Learning.

Kotusev, S. (2019). Enterprise architecture and enterprise architecture artifacts: Questioning the old concept in light of new findings. *Journal of Information Technology*, *34*(2), 102–128. https://doi.org/10.1177/0268396218816273

Microsoft Singapore. (2020, December 28). *AIA group limited technical story*. Microsoft. https://customers.microsoft.com/en-us/story/860509-aia-singapore-drives-performance-enhancements-after-moving-java-applications-to-azure

Niemi, E., & Pekkola, S. (2016). Enterprise architecture benefit realization: Review of the models and a case study of a public organization. *The Data Base for Advances in Information Systems*, *47*(3), 55–80. https://doi.org/10.1145/2980783.2980787

Open Group. (2018). *The TOGAF standard version 9.2: A standard of the open group*. The Open Group.

Perez-Castillo, R., Ruiz, F., Piattini, M., & Ebert, C. (2019). Enterprise architecture. *IEEE Software*, *36*(4), 12–19. https://doi.org/10.1109/MS.2019.2909329

Shanks, G., Gloet, M., Asadi Someh, I., Frampton, K., & Tamm, T. (2018). Achieving benefits with enterprise architecture. *The Journal of Strategic Information Systems*, *27*(2), 139–156. https://doi.org/10.1016/j.jsis.2018.03.001

8

Business Applications of Digital Technology

At least 40% of all businesses will die in the next 10 years... if they don't figure out how to change their entire company to accommodate new technologies.

John Chambers, Cisco Systems

UNLOCKING LIMITLESS POSSIBILITIES

Advanced technology has always fired humankind's imagination about future possibilities. Like in many science fiction movies and novels, technology opens many opportunities to do things differently. Likewise, technology has been playing a key enabling role in digital transformation. It has unlocked numerous possibilities for enhancing operations and delighting customers. Organizations can significantly improve operating efficiency and increase productivity using digital technologies. These technologies can also help organizations to innovate and create new business models.

There are many types of digital technologies available to the organization today. These new and emerging technologies offer a wide range of business applications for organization to digitally transform and deliver radical change. Some of these business applications include miniaturization of devices, mechanization of processes, virtualization of hardware, personalization by software applications, and monetization of data. While using information technology (IT) to create competitive advantage is not something new, it is the integration of all these digital components to almost every aspect of the organization's value chain that makes digital transformation distinctive from previous forms of IT-enabled change (Furr & Shipilov, 2019). However, organizations must be careful about technology hype and fads. There are many instances of failed promises. Ultimately, the main purpose for introducing any form of digital technologies to the organization is to close business gaps and derive value for the customers. Organizations must select the appropriate digital technology and apply it to the correct business scenario to achieve the desired results. The digital technology per se is not the main differentiator for competitiveness. The technology that is available to the organization can also be easily accessible by others. Therefore, it is how the organization deploys it that will make the key difference. The key consideration is in the application of technology to solve business problems.

Digital technology is constantly evolving, and it is a challenge to keep up to date on the latest developments. Nevertheless, one should develop a good understanding of enabling digital technologies, trends, and business applications, also to acquire some basic knowledge of use cases on how these digital technologies impact business, government, and society. Some of the more popular digital technologies include artificial intelligence (AI), big data analytics, Internet of Things (IoT), wearables, augmented reality (AR), social media, robotic process automation (RPA), and cybersecurity.

ARTIFICIAL INTELLIGENCE

Human intelligence covers many facets and includes cognitive and behavioral processes. Through these abilities, human beings can learn from the external environment and make appropriate responses to any changes. Artificial intelligence attempts to imitate these capabilities in computers using logic and decision rules. These computers can carry out activities in the way considered intelligent by humans. They do so by following human decision-making processes. AI strives to be more human-like by applying techniques that allow computers to learn from and recommend actions based on collected data. AI consists of a large body of knowledge that has undergone various cycles of 'highs' and 'lows'. The standard topics covered include feature engineering, probability theory, regression methods, and neural networks. Two AI-related terms are machine learning and deep learning. Machine learning is a subset of AI, where statistical techniques and data are applied to improve task performance and outcomes.

Basically, instead of being taught by humans, computers learn by them-selves by going through massive amounts of data to perform the tasks. Deep learning models mimic how the human brain works and use neural networks as the basis for learning new information.

One application of AI harnesses its capability to examine massive num-ber of documents and provide a trend analysis. For example, court judg-ment reports and medical history records can be gathered and analyzed. With some keywords search, legal and medical professionals can easily find sentencing of precedent cases and clinical diagnosis of specific infec-tions. In such cases, the AI recommendations can be quite like those offered by experts in these fields. In business, AI enables organizations to view each customer as an individual and recommend specific products and services to meet their needs. With the customer data gathered, the organization can create a personalized experience with more accurate information and relevant products and services to them. AI can build a profile for each customer based on the collected data and customize a unique plan. This is a key differentiator among competitors which can only offer standard solutions.

Recent successes such as AlphaGo have once again given AI another boost. However, there are still much work to be done to make machines more human-like. Some common challenges include accessibility to large data sets and algorithmic bias (Chui et al., 2018). AI uses data repeatedly to build algorithms. For it to be effective, a lot of data records is required to 'train' the system so that tasks can be classified, and decision rules can be established. As an example, for a computer to recognize an object such as a chair, it will require thousands of pictures and pattern recognition rules for it to 'learn'. Similarly, thousands or millions of kilometers on the road are required for analysis before an autonomous vehicle can navigate on its own without a human driver. Unfortunately, in many instances, it is not possible to obtain sufficiently large data points. The ability to drill down to a deeper level of the information is important in correlation anal-ysis. If the information is inadequate, the algorithms or decision rules gen-erated will be skewed toward certain outcomes. Thus, the data records should also be comprehensive so that more details can be uncovered should the situations arise. For example, if the data collection of job recruitment applications is uneven across age groups, with some groups having a higher representation and others with zero returns, then prob-lems will surface in the analysis and predictions. Such systematic errors will lead to algorithmic bias. Therefore, a researcher must be very careful in the selection of data and recognize any underlying assumptions in the model design.

Natural language processing (NLP) is another concept that is related to AI. It is concerned with how computers deal with human speech or writing without having to conform to strict programming language requirements. In other words, a person can speak or write in the natural form and the computers will be able to translate the information, analyze it, and respond accordingly. While this seems like a very straightforward process, it is a big challenge to perform even a very simple natural language task. The reason is that the human language has many linguistic nuances such as dialects and slangs. Together with other language parameters such as syntax and context, it becomes increasingly complex to develop products such as voice recognition and speech-to-text applications.

An emerging digital technology area is the use of quantum computers for machine learning. Compared to conventional computers, quantum computers can search for many more solutions to a computing problem at once. To achieve this, quantum computing uses qubits that can store data in a much more complex state that combines both 0 and 1. Traditional computers can only store data as bits that can be either a 0 or a 1. The application of quantum computing is very useful in industries such as banking and finance, and logistics because it can solve optimization problems with large amounts of data and at many times the speed compared to conventional computers.

BIG DATA ANALYTICS

Data has been touted as the new oil of the digital era. In the early days of the internet, humans create data mainly through inputs into computers and machines. In the present day, there is a huge increase in the amount of digital information being generated, stored, and made available for analysis. Myriads of applications and devices continuously generate data every single minute. The exponential growth of data is expected to continue in the years to come. This phenomenon leads to what the market calls big data. Big data entails an enormous data set. To qualify for the definition of big data, some characteristics have been identified (Sivarajah et al., 2017). A common set of attributes involves the five 'Vs', namely, volume, velocity, variety, variability, and veracity. Volume refers to the amount of data generated which the unit of measurement has been increasing from gigabytes to zettabytes, and beyond. Velocity refers to the speed of new data generation and transmission. Variety deals with the different types of data that are available for use. Variability means that the data itself is constantly changing. Finally, veracity defines the level of accuracy or trustworthiness of the data. In some definitions, the number of characteristics has even been expanded to include visualization and value. These data come in many forms such as structured data, unstructured data, and semi-structured data. Briefly, structured data such as credit card names have a defined length and format while unstructured data such as photographs do not follow a specified format. Semi-structured data such as delimited files fall between these two forms of data.

Data analytics is applied to provide answers to business problems. There are four types of analytics used by organizations that bring about different types of value depending on the type of business questions raised (Aggarwal, 2021; Erl et al., 2016). They are descriptive, diagnostic, predictive, and prescriptive analytics. Descriptive analytics summarizes existing data and presents the historical information on what has occurred. A sample question would be 'What was the monthly subscription revenue over the past three years?' Diagnostic analytics builds on knowledge of past information and attempts to find out the cause of an event. An example of this type of question would be 'Why was there a decrease in the number of tourist arrivals over the last quarter?' Predictive analytics is more forward looking as it tries to forecast possible future outcomes using statistical techniques. A relevant question would be 'What is the likelihood of a customer purchasing an extended warranty with this television model?' Finally, prescriptive analytics can recommend a course of action or alternatives after analyzing the data. An illustrative question would be 'What should the robot do when the pathway is blocked?' The business applications of data analytics are many and varied. For example, online retailers use recommender systems to suggest products and services to customers. In banking and finance, fraud detection applications are used to identify any malicious actions whenever money is transacted across dubious accounts. Similarly, insurance organizations employ predictive risk modeling based on demographic and geographic indicators to assess applications for insurance products to balance between the premiums offered and risk profiles.

Some of the main challenges related to data faced by organizations today are multiple data sources within the organization and the misinterpretation of data. Very often, data is collected and stored by multiple departments in an organization. This forms a natural boundary which limits access to data. Multiple data sources also create other problems such as difficulties in confirming the veracity of data. The variety of data and its sources also make data integration more complicated because these data may not be compatible. Consequently, the business insights that can be derived from data analysis will be significantly reduced. To resolve this issue, some organizations have tried to organize all the available data by creating a 'data lake'. This centralized repository can store vast amounts of raw structured and unstructured data that can be used for later analysis. Having such a singular data storage solution will be beneficial in the upkeep of data across the organization. Another major concern in business analytics is around the confusion between causation and correlation. A common business question asked is 'What is the effect of event A on event B?' In the case of causation, which is about cause and effect, an event occurred as a direct result of another event happening. On the other hand, correlation means that both events happened at the same time. It does not imply that the occurrence of the event was the result of another event. In simple language, the event did not happen automatically because of another event happening. Thus, organizations need to be very careful in their trials. Ideally, a controlled experiment in which a sample is divided into two groups with comparable attributes should be conducted. Then, different interventions can be applied to the two groups and the outcomes compared to determine possible cause and effect.

INTERNET OF THINGS

In the early internet days, few physical devices tapped on the cyberspace and were connected to one another. Over time, more and more gadgets are developed to form a group of interconnected devices on the World Wide Web. This network of interconnected devices with sensors on the internet is referred to as the Internet of Things. Technically, any physical devices ranging from wearables, robots, drones, to vending machines can be included. However, IoT is not merely just a collection of linked physical devices. It is usually combined with other hardware and software to analyze large volumes of data collected from operations. In more advanced cases, IoT may lead to new business model innovations such as servitization (Haaker et al., 2021). IoT has a wide range of applications across many sectors. In healthcare, patients who require health monitoring can put on wearables so that vital statistics such as heart rate, blood pressure, and body temperature can be tracked 24/7. A key benefit of IoT is that it allows remote monitoring so that patients can stay at home and do not need to be physically located in a hospital. In the building sector, smart offices that are IoT-enabled can actively monitor and analyze key areas such as energy utilization, security, and fire detection.

Despite the proliferation of IoT, some organizations are still holding from full implementation of this technology. For instance, organizations need to be careful in the selection of IoT products and services. There are several wireless standards for networked devices with many proprietary ones in the current industry. The development of these standards is still ongoing. In addition, there are other technical issues to be addressed such as battery life of the device and operating systems for the accompanying software. There may also be other reasons which prevent IoT adoption in organizations. For example, a perceived high cost in the purchase of sensors, the inability to pinpoint the business value for installation, and uncertainties in IT security arising from a sensor network. One approach to hasten IoT adoption is for the organizations to work with a vendor to initiate a pilot project within a specific business area or operation. By collaborating with an experienced partner on a small initiative, executive management will gain insights and develop greater confidence from the lessons learned. With this experience, a larger scale exercise can be planned and executed.

WEARABLES

Wearables as a form of technology offer a distinct advantage over others as it allows for hands-free workflow and access to information. Users can view real-time information with minimal interruptions to their current activities. Wearables enhance business activities because they allow users to complete their task faster and more efficiently. Organizations will be able to streamline business processes and shorten turnaround time without lowering service quality. Broadly, wearables refer to easy-to-wear mobile devices with wireless communications capability (Luczak et al.,

2020). The wearables market covers an extensive wide range of products such as smart watches, smart glasses, wearable cameras, and smart clothing (Ometov et al., 2021). The sports and fitness, healthcare, construction, and logistics sectors are some of the major consumers of wearables technology. With a wearable device, individuals can very easily monitor their health by downloading a mobile application. The fitness tracker will measure patterns of activity such as the number of steps taken and sleep cycle. The main purpose is to encourage proactive healthcare through real-time tracking. Athletes can determine the distance covered through the global positioning system (GPS) and adjust the training intensity program accordingly based on the heart rate achieved. Similarly, in a healthcare setting, nurses can actively monitor vital signs such as electrocardiogram, blood pressure, and temperature if the patient dons a wearable device. When signs of distress are detected, alerts will be activated to inform the healthcare team. In emergency cases, early detection saves lives because the span of a few seconds could mean life or death.

Wearables also have a wide application in the industrial context and contribute significantly to workplace safety (Svertoka et al., 2021). For employees working in a high-risk or enclosed environment, putting on a wearable device will enable a senior colleague to be able to provide remote guidance in the operations. Through the wearable, the off-site expert can view the surroundings and assist the on-site personnel to identify and rectify any unusual problems in real time. If a hazard such as fire or gas leak does occur, the employee can also be alerted through a wearable device. Doing so not only raises work productivity but, more importantly, improves safety standards by preventing accidents from happening. In a logistics warehouse, employees must constantly move around the facility to receive and ship out goods. In the process, also to control inventory and perform other administrative tasks. With the aid of a wearable gadget, the employee can obtain and transmit real-time inventory data without having to be stationed at a fixed workstation to get the job done. Furthermore, if the employee is supported by smart glasses with AR features, then locating the specific items becomes a great deal easier since the AR will be able to direct the user to the place where the item is stored. One can imagine the productivity gained especially during peak seasons and when operating a big warehouse.

As a digital technology that people put on their body, comfort is a key consideration for widespread adoption. Wearable devices should be designed for wearing comfort over an extended period. The person should not constantly feel or be reminded that a wearable device is fitted to the body. Just like the clothes and glasses one wears; a wearable device should not bring about any discomfort and make one conscious of its existence. Thus, ergonomics and choice of material of the wearable device are important factors to ensure its continued and long-term use.

AUGMENTED REALITY

Augmented reality and virtual reality (VR) are two common forms of immersive technology. AR enhances real-world objects with computer-generated simulations while VR creates a totally artificial environment for the user (Soliman et al., 2017). Mixed reality (MR) is a combination of AR and VR where real and virtual world contents can interact with each other. The key feature is that digital technology can build unique personalized experiences by blending the physical and digital worlds through computer simulations. With advances in AR and VR innovations, there is widespread adoption of these applications in areas such as occupational therapy (Suh & Prophet, 2018). Hospitals employ AR and VR technologies to provide remote case support as part of the healthcare ecosystem. Patients undergoing physiotherapy can perform rehabilitative exercises using computer simulations and receive guidance from allied health professionals in the comfort of their homes. In the education sector, AR and VR can help hearing-impaired children to improve sign language skills through gamification. Essentially, the children wear motion-sensing gloves and interact with virtual cartoon characters on the computer. The system will recognize the correct gestures and reward the user with points to upgrade the level of the animated cartoon character. AR can also offer a more exciting and interesting shopping experience. Through AR and data analytics, organizations can introduce interactive location awareness features, product demonstrations, and personalized advertisements to enhance customer experience.

While the use cases seemed to suggest that immersive technology has a positive effect on physical and cognitive performance, there are also disadvantages related to the use of AR and VR. For example, some users may experience symptoms such as dizziness, headaches, and nausea when staring at a monitor over a prolonged period. Also, the associated activities usually require the user to put on a wearable such as a headset or visor. The additional weight of these physical accessories brings much discomfort to the user and will aggravate the symptoms. Notwithstanding these limitations, immersive technology does offer much potential to transform user experience. Organizations which adopt AR and VR applications can develop new and personalized experiences for the customers. Virtual simulations enable users to break away from the routines in a safe virtual environment. For organizations intending to deploy immersive technology solutions, it is important to work in close collaboration with key stakeholders to ensure a seamless process transitioning between the physical and digital environment and a quality outcome.

SOCIAL MEDIA

Social media refers to applications that support the creation and distribution of information for building communities. These communities may be businesses or consumers. On the internet, the requirements of transacting with businesses and consumers differ greatly between the two groups (Nikolinakou & Phua, 2020). Thus, it is very important to develop a good understanding of their motivations in sharing content.

Many organizations have been very successful in using social media to reach out to their customers. Through a social media platform, an organization can identify the target customer segments based on demographic and psychographic characteristics. With key insights into customer preferences, the organization can provide personalized products and services to them. They can advertise products and services for a target customer segment by pushing relevant content to specific interest groups on the social media platform. Potential customers will receive information that is more applicable to them. In addition, organizations can effectively generate more leads and at the same time incur a lower transaction cost through these social media platforms. This is because of the availability of information on customer profiles and interests that are associated with social groups. By tapping on social media, organizations can better understand customer behaviors and improve customer engagement (Dolan et al., 2019). Having a deep knowledge of the customer and the ability to meet the individual's needs is a key competitive advantage for any organization. The organization will be able to build up long-lasting relationships with the customers and create customer stickiness through recurring transactions and repeat purchases.

There is a growing concern over how organizations are using personal data. Organizations obtain different types of personal data of their customers through business transactions. These personal data range from basic identifiers such as names and home addresses to more sensitive information such as national identification numbers. With information and communications technology, huge volumes of personal data can be effortlessly collected, stored, and used. Depending on the purpose in which these personal data are being used, ethical and legal issues may arise. An example of a misuse of personal data is the sale of these information to third-party advertisers. To prevent any form of abuse, many jurisdictions have started to implement in phases personal data protection legislations and policies. Therefore, organizations must be careful in managing personal data. Any form of mishandling will result in an infringement of personal privacy. Organizations must ensure that customers' personal data are appropriately handled by authorized staff, securely stored in the systems, and not to be used for any other purposes without prior consent from the individuals. Furthermore, the organization must conduct regular reviews of data policies and access to safeguard the security and privacy of information.

ROBOTIC PROCESS AUTOMATION

Organizations very often must cope with problems arising from outdated manual workflows. These redundant activities increase the turnaround time and create unnecessary errors. One approach in addressing these business process issues is to redesign the process. A process redesign involves a review of the activities performed, the information flow, and the roles concerned. A review of the activities includes examining the number of steps required to accomplish the tasks, the transaction volume, and the number of customers served. A review of the information flow covers the difficulties encountered in the collection, dissemination, and utilization of data. Finally, a role analysis is performed to ascertain the number of employees and workload involved in completing the various tasks. To further improve efficiency and effectiveness, organization can turn to robotic process automation. RPA solutions are superior to traditional workflow automation tools because they can learn directly from a user performing a set of tasks and repeat those tasks without having to write the codes. There are several benefits to the organization in adopting RPA. Cost savings is a major advantage. The manpower that is used to work on the previous paper-based workflow can be re-deployed to the other areas of work. Furthermore, the new RPA solutions usually provide better integration with backup systems, thereby, enhancing overall IT performance.

CYBERSECURITY

In the digital world, cybersecurity is a necessity. Organizations must ensure that their digital and physical assets are protected from malicious hacking activities. While most of the organizations focused on the defensive aspects of cybersecurity, some have embarked on a different path. Instead of defense, these organizations adopt an attack stance. In other words, they apply offensive techniques to hunt down cyber threats before an attack takes place. Sophisticated analytics-driven threat hunting tools are used to reveal cyber adversaries on the networks and neutralize these threats. Besides using digital technology to combat cyber threats, the organization also needs to institutionalize digital governance processes to support the work of the IT security team. Executive management must take an active role to direct the appropriate resources to counter cyber threats. It takes years of effort to build a successful digital platform business but only a few moments for it to fall apart because of a breach of security.

CASE ILLUSTRATION

With the advancement and pervasiveness of digital technologies, physical objects and processes can be replicated to create a digital twin (Mussomeli et al., 2018). This is made possible through digital technologies such as IoT sensors and AR. Data are collected from the ground and used to build digital replicas. By building a virtual model of the real thing, simulations can be conducted, and insights gained to improve operations based on different scenarios. Organizations would be able to make model-driven decisions and apply the changes to the original system with lower risk and better return on investment. Various Singapore government agencies have been collaborating to develop a dynamic three-dimensional model of the city. When the Virtual Singapore project is completed, stakeholders from different sectors will be able to deploy applications for test-bedding concepts and services (National Research Foundation Singapore, 2020). This would help in the planning, decision-making, and deployment of solutions to solve complex urban challenges such as traffic congestion, overcrowding, and solar energy integration in the city state (JTC Corporation, 2021; Lim, 2021).

SUMMARY

This chapter highlights the many possibilities offered by digital technology for digital transformation. A list of digital technologies is described along with the business applications. These digital technologies include artificial intelligence, big data analytics, IoT, wearables, augmented reality, social media, robotic process automation, and cybersecurity. Artificial intelligence attempts to imitate human capabilities in computers using logic and decision. Big data analytics entails analyzing an enormous data set to derive customer insights. IoT taps on the strengths of a network of sensors to collect and analyze data. Wearables enable the monitoring of real-time data for human beings. Augmented reality provides a great opportunity to fuse objects in the physical and digital worlds. Social media promotes interaction and exchange of information. Robotic process automation helps to significantly reduce the amount of manual and repetitive work, thereby, raising productivity. Also, advances in cybersecurity enable a more proactive way to defend the organization against malicious attacks.

REFERENCES

Aggarwal, S. (2021). *What is business analytics? Definition, examples & types*. Great Learning. https://www.mygreatlearning.com/blog/what-is-business-analytics/

Chui, M., Manyika, J., & Miremadi, M. (2018). *What AI can and can't do (yet) for your business*. McKinsey Quarterly. https://www.mckinsey.com/business-functions/mckinsey-analytics/our-insights/what-ai-can-and-cant-do-yet-for-your-business#

Dolan, R., Conduit, J., Frethey-Bentham, C., Fahy, J., & Goodman, S. (2019). Social media engagement behavior: A framework for engaging customers through social media content. *European Journal of Marketing, 53*(10), 2213–2243. https://doi.org/10.1108/EJM-03-2017-0182

Erl, T., Khattak, W., & Buhler, P. (2016). *Big data fundamentals: Concepts, drivers & techniques.* Prentice Hall, ServiceTech Press.

Furr, N., & Shipilov, A. (2019). *Digital doesn't have to be disruptive.* Harvard Business Review. https://hbr.org/2019/07/digital-doesnt-have-to-be-disruptive

Haaker, T., Ly, P. T. M., Nguyen-Thanh, N., & Nguyen, H. T. H. (2021). Business model innovation through the application of the Internet-of-Things: A comparative analysis. *Journal of Business Research, 126,* 126–136. https://doi.org/10.1016/j.jbusres.2020.12.034

JTC Corporation. (2021, August 31). *Open digital platform: The digital backbone of Punggol digital district.* Government of Singapore. https://estates.jtc.gov.sg/pdd/stories/open-digital-platform-the-digital-backbone-of-pdd

Lim, V. (2021, October 27). *New 'digital twin' for national power grid to better manage Singapore's electricity supply.* Channel News Asia. https://www.channelnewsasia.com/singapore/new-digital-twin-national-power-grid-manage-electricity-supply-2271356

Luczak, T., Burch, R., Lewis, E., Chander, H., & Ball, J. (2020). State-of-the-art review of athletic wearable technology: What 113 strength and conditioning coaches and athletic trainers from the USA said about technology in sports. *International Journal of Sports Science & Coaching, 15*(1), 26–40. https://doi.org/10.1177/1747954119885244

Mussomeli, A., Meeker, B., Shepley, S. & Schatsky, D. (2018). *Expecting digital twins: Adoption of these versatile avatars is spreading across industries.* Deloitte Insights. https://www2.deloitte.com/content/dam/insights/us/articles/3773_Expecting-digital-twins/DI_Expecting-digital-twins.pdf

National Research Foundation Singapore. (2020). *Virtual Singapore.* https://www.nrf.gov.sg/programmes/virtual-singapore

Nikolinakou, A., & Phua, J. (2020). Do human values matter for promoting brands on social media? How social media users' values influence valuable brand-related activities such as sharing, content creation, and reviews. *Journal of Consumer Behaviour, 19*(1), 13–23. https://doi.org/10.1002/cb.1790

Ometov, A., Shubina, V., Klus, L., Skibińska, J., Saafi, S., Pascacio, P., Flueratoru, L., Gaibor, D. Q., Chukhno, N., Chukhno, O., Ali, A., Channa, A., Svertoka, E., Qaim, W. B., Casanova-Marqués, R., Holcer, S., Torres-Sospedra, J., Casteleyn, S., Ruggeri, G., ... Lohan, E. S. (2021). A survey on wearable technology: history, state-of-the-art and current challenges. *Computer Networks (Amsterdam, Netherlands: 1999), 193,* 108074. https://doi.org/10.1016/j.comnet.2021.108074

Sivarajah, U., Kamal, M. M., Irani, Z., & Weerakkody, V. (2017). Critical analysis of Big Data challenges and analytical methods. *Journal of Business Research, 70,* 263–286. https://doi.org/10.1016/j.jbusres.2016.08.001

Soliman, M., Peetz, J., & Davydenko, M. (2017). The impact of immersive technology on nature relatedness and pro-environmental behavior. *Journal of Media Psychology: Theories, Methods, and Applications, 29*(1), 8–17. https://doi.org/10.1027/1864-1105/a000213

Suh, A., & Prophet, J. (2018). The state of immersive technology research: A literature analysis. *Computers in Human Behavior, 86*, 77–90. https://doi.org/10.1016/j.chb. 2018.04.019

Svertoka, E., Saafi, S., Rusu-Casandra, A., Burget, R., Marghescu, I., Hosek, J., & Ometov, A. (2021). Wearables for industrial work safety: A survey. *Sensors (Basel, Switzerland), 21*(11), 3844. https://doi.org/10.3390/s21113844

Conclusion

We're only at the very, very beginning of this next generation of computing and I think that every industry leader will be the ones that transform first. I don't care what industry you're talking about.

Kim Stevenson, Lenovo

UNDERSTANDING THE BUILDING BLOCKS

Over the years, digital transformation has taken center stage for many organizations in the region and around the world. There are many reasons for this phenomenon. On the demand side, changing demographics has led to a significant rise in the number of digital natives who are savvy internet and mobile device users. Many communities which are spread over large geographical distances can now become more connected with the introduction of digital technologies. On the supply side, existing digital technologies have matured with many of the initial technical problems resolved. Furthermore, the business climate has also changed dramatically particularly with the COVID-19 pandemic. Industry boundaries are constantly being redefined. Today, organizations require go-to-market strategies that have a much shorter time frame and cover a larger scope. With all these factors taken together, organizations have no choice but to embark on a journey of digital transformation. They need to innovate and re-invent their existing business models for competitive advantage. Many of these organizations have pledged to accelerate Industry 4.0 transformation through digital technologies such as cloud computing and artificial intelligence.

Traditionally, organizations rely on a set of established methodologies and external best practices to address innovation gaps. They either replicate

DOI: 10.1201/9781003311393-10

these popular techniques or incorporate others established procedures into their business and operating models. It is a structured and linear way to improve the organization. However, in the digital age, these frequently used and well-tested approaches are no longer effective to bring about quantum leap results. The conventional linear pattern of doing business where products and services move through a value chain from producers to sellers to customers is transitioning into a circular business model consisting of digital platforms, networks, and ecosystems. With these changes, it is no longer sufficient to discover breakthrough ideas simply by using standard templates and checklists. Organizations need to explore different approaches to innovate as part of the digital transformation journey. They also need to understand the building blocks that are necessary for creating the right conditions for digital transformation to happen.

Digital transformation is a multi-dimensional concept and requires various building blocks. In the broadest sense, it involves changing the way business is done enabled by digital technologies. Thus, to successfully navigate in the digital landscape, an organization needs to, first and foremost, return to the basics of understanding the real business problem. This means taking a customer's point of view and creating an outcome-based solution to delight the customer. The digital transformation strategy may involve creating a digital platform in an ecosystem to provide seamless end-to-end experience for the customers. To enable more responsive decision-making, the organization should review its digital governance and risk management frameworks and also, to mobilize the people in the organization toward a shared vision. This involves articulating what it means to be a digital organization and developing a structured change management program. To further augment execution, the organization could introduce practices in areas such as experimental learning and design thinking, digital product management, Agile and DevSecOps, and digital enterprise architecture. Finally, organizational processes should be designed around the customer with the appropriate digital technologies and data applied to enhance engagement.

DEVELOPING DIGITAL COMPETENCIES

In the ever-changing world of digital technologies, organizations not only have to keep pace with emerging digital trends but also need to constantly develop the relevant digital capabilities to solve complex problems. These digital capabilities must go beyond simply achieving productivity gains for the organization. Instead, they should enable the organization to create business value through innovations. To develop and strengthen organizational capabilities, the organization must develop a strong pool of digital talents and train individuals and teams in the various digital competencies. The organization should begin developing digital competencies at the individual level then progress to the team level. As more individuals develop new digital competencies and contribute to the groups, the organization would be better positioned to compete in the digital world. However, it is important that the employees themselves take ownership of their learning and gain higher proficiency in their respective areas of work.

To excel in digital transformation, an individual should have a blend of both business and information technology (IT) competencies. When either one of these areas is missing, it would hamper an individual's ability to create a complete and effective digital solution to deliver business value. For illustration, a business-savvy individual without the appropriate technical knowledge may find it extremely difficult to clearly articulate a business problem at a level of details which the technical team can understand and translate the requirements into a technological solution. Conversely, an individual with a very strong technical background may find it a challenge to effectively develop a digital solution which addresses a real business gap. Thus, in the ideal scenario, an individual should be trained in both business and IT domains. However, in practice, it is difficult to recruit such individuals who are both business-savvy and technically strong. To close this talent gap, training could be provided to help individuals who are competent in one area to be cross trained in another area. In the digital context, it means developing a holistic set of competencies which cover both business and IT domains. Essentially, the key outcomes are to produce digital talents who can synthesize information across domains and interact with domain specialists. Also, the training must help individuals look at issues holistically from different perspectives and understand how things really work.

At the team level, the main goal should be to achieve work synergies among individuals. Cross-functional groups could be formed to identify complex business issues and develop end-to-end digital solutions. When groups of competent individuals can work closely together to solve problems, then the organization benefits from this collective capability. At the organization level, executive management could create an environment where employees can easily participate in learning. For example, short talks on a digital technology topic by invited external speakers or in-house specialists can be organized during office hours or lunch breaks. This would make it more convenient for employees to acquire new knowledge. Regardless of whether it is formal or informal training, the main purpose is to help employees constantly reexamine existing assumptions on the way they conduct their daily business so that organization can progress.

FINAL THOUGHTS

Although the constantly evolving market environment and fast-moving digital technologies have caused numerous disruptions across industries and sectors, they have also presented many business opportunities along the way. To thrive in the digital era, organizations must be more agile and innovative in dealing with the customers. The individuals must be equipped with the necessary digital competencies to make things happen. Therefore, an important attribute to stay competitive is to be always ready to adopt new mindsets and look at issues from a fresh perspective. Only by changing the way one thinks and approaches a challenge can one hope to achieve breakthrough results in digital transformation.

Index

Printed in the United States
by Baker & Taylor Publisher Services